THE IMPORTANCE BEING PETER

Carsten Clovelly

Copyright Carsten Clovelly 2025.

Carsten Clovelly asserts the moral right to be identified as the author of this work.

This novel is entirely a work of fiction.

The names, characters and incidents portrayed in it are the work of the author's imagination. Any resemblance to actual persons living or dead, business establishments, events, or locales is purely coincidental.

All rights reserved. No part of this publication may be reproduced, stored in a retrieval system, or transmitted, in any form or by any means, electronic, mechanical, photocopying, recording or otherwise, without the prior permission of the author.

Use of this work to train generative AI is strictly prohibited.

This book is sold subject to the conditions that it shall not, by way of trade or otherwise, be lent, re-sold, hired out, or otherwise circulated without the author's prior consent in any form of binding or cover other than in which it is published and without a similar condition including this condition being imposed on the subsequent publisher.

This book is for Moriarty. (Bribiba Inspiration) 21.05.2016 to 13.01.2025.

My assistance dog, psychoanalyst and friend.

Table of Contents

Chapter 1 Rogue Male

Chapter 2 The Rainbow Thief

Chapter 3 What's New Pussycat

Chapter 4 How to Steal a Million

Chapter 5 Wings of Fame

Chapter 6 The Final Curtain

Chapter 7 Bright Young Things

Chapter 8 Stardust

Chapter 9 High Spirits

Chapter 10 Sherlock Holmes and the Valley of Fear

Chapter 11 Fairytale, a True Story

Chapter 12 How to Steal a Million (Reprise)

Chapter 13 Jeffery Bernard is Unwell

Chapter 14 The Lion in Winter

Chapter 15 Goodbye Mr Chips

Chapter 16 Christmas Cottage

Chapter 17 My Talks with Dean Spanley

Chapter 18 Country Dance

Chapter 19 Power Play

Chapter 20 Heavy Weather

Chapter 21 Man of La Mancha

Chapter 22 Venus

Chapter 23 Great Catherine

Chapter 24 The Ruling Class

Chapter 25 My Favourite Year

Chapter 26 Lord Jim

Chapter 27 Becket

Chapter 28 Masada

Preface

This book started as a dream, then the narrative kept building in my head as the days went by. Eventually I wrote it down to clear the log jam of words in my brain. When I started, Moriarty inserted himself into the tale. Although he had not been there in my imagination at the start, it soon became clear he was vital to the tale. Having completed it my overactive synapses started work on a sequel.

Acknowledgments

Who do I need to thank?

Firstly, my long-suffering wife who took on the onerous task of editing my appalling spelling and grammar. The joys of being married to a dyslexic author.

Thanks to Fran & Bill Barnbrook of Bribiba Wolfhounds. They gave us Moriarty. He was a joy and an inspiration.

My cover artist Daniel Greenhalgh for his excellent work and advice. Thank you for all that.

Lastly, Em (Emily) Buchanan, my talented daughter-in-law. The famous author of "Send Flowers", she was invaluable with all her advice and encouragement.

Chapter 1

ROGUE MALE

Nathan clung with desperate waning strength to the rope; his arms and shoulders were burning and cramping with fatigue. The gentle night-time breeze slowly rotated him. A dope on a rope. The mellow yellow of the sandstone blocks slid past his vision. Next the glittering lights of London, scattered like diamonds on black velvet, hove into view.

Far below in the alley, locked in the van, Moriarty looked on in helpless horror. He could only watch as the man who was closer to him than a brother, dangled, perilously suspended, certain death beckoning.

Nathan considered the mortifying fact that he was so tired he lacked the power to either ascend or descend. Being three floors up, he realised that while the fall would not kill him, stopping at the bottom most definitely would. How had he got himself stuck in this ridiculous situation? Sadly, the answer was all too obvious. It was all his own fault. There really was no one else to blame. His brain started to explore all the different scenarios that might just hold the rescue plan for his current predicament, but the only things he could bring to mind were all the events that had occurred during this madcap quest he had started almost twelve months ago.

* * *

The Beginning:

The Suffolk seaside town of Southwold baked gently in the shimmering heat of a late July morning. Dogs slept gratefully in the shade, legs twitching in pursuit of dream rabbits. Cats sprawled in the sunlight in warm abandon. Seagulls strutted insolently in search of lost chips. Even the summer visitors thronging the promenade and pier wandered in a lazy daze of sun kissed torpor. The sea hissed and whispered its secrets in languid swells over the smooth spherical flints of the beach. Brightly painted beach huts greeted the breeze along the lower promenade. Along the upper-level, Georgian houses gazed out with blind eyes across the offing. The bold exclamation mark of the vintage pier thrust its length out over the water. This was a town that defied the hustle and bustle of today's life; permanently encased in an antique glaze, it rejected the modern world.

Nathan Stockwood, a moderately successful actor, was currently enjoying a short break from his latest engagement. He sat in his favourite seat, in his favourite corner, in his favourite pub. He was sprawled on a high-backed settle. The wood of the seat was worn to that silky-smooth patina only achieved by generations of patrons. It was situated in the sweet spot that was close enough to the window for enough light to read, and yet far enough away from the log fire so your legs didn't burn in winter. Before him on the table a pint of Adnams beer from the local brewery sat; its smooth glassy exterior beaded with glistening drops of dew. Alongside that a copy of the Times and the latest edition of The Stage: both journals were vital to his morning regime.

The Times was there primarily for the crossword; he gave the news items no more than a cursory glance, having little or no interest in the state of an obviously insane and declining world. However, he prided himself that he always completed the crossword. Often, he would however, have to resort to a unique mental exercise of his own devising to finish it. Having reached the point at which he could no longer supply the set answers, he had to search his mind for words that would fit the vacant spaces. This achieved two goals. Firstly, anyone passing or seated nearby, spotting a completed Times crossword, would be impressed by his breadth of knowledge and his intellect. Secondly, it exercised his mind to extract words from the storehouse of his vocabulary. This he considered an excellent challenge for any professional actor, since words were the tools in his workshop. It was also vital that this task was completed in pen. Not for him the fainthearted use of a pencil; that just betrayed a lack of confidence.

The Stage was primarily purchased for any intrigue and Situations Vacant; gossip being the lifeblood of any actor. The victories, and especially the failures of his peers, were meat and drink to him. The Situations Vacant section was not strictly essential, but from time to time it provided some part he might feel worth auditioning for, simply because he liked the part, or the company, or the director. His moderate success meant that while he was one of those actors you recognised, you could not always remember his name. He was in his mid-forties. His height was a little over six feet tall. He presented a slim, vaguely athletic build, that took no effort whatsoever to maintain. This was coupled with fine aristocratic features. As a result, he was pleasing to the eye, whether on stage or screen. In addition to this his slow, faintly upper-class refined drawl was perfect for the second leading man in dramas and comedies on stage. His looks, reliability and talent meant he was also a regular on the small screen, often being cast in a variety of dramas. He was particularly popular with the casting directors of murder mysteries: the type that feature eccentric, troubled detectives who drive vintage cars, have a love for one specific type of music, usually either jazz or classical, and invariably very unlucky in love. It was a given that any romantic interest in the story will automatically prove to be the murderer.

Next to him, also perched on the settle, was Moriarty. At first this may not sound particularly noteworthy. However, Moriarty is a dog. Not just any dog but an Irish wolfhound of such prodigious size, that it was his custom to back up to chairs and sit in them. He had developed this habit because as far as he was concerned both he and Nathan, while anatomically different, were the same species. If Nathan sat that way, then so would he. The major difference being that when he sat, he still had all four feet on the floor. Moriarty was a large, powerful, untidy looking wolfhound of the finest breeding, and like all true aristocrats he was somewhat unfussy about his general appearance. That, and his distinct aversion to being brushed gave him a wild, and in his opinion romantically tousled look. He had once heard it described as "windswept and interesting." He was quite happy to be bathed from time to time, so that his aroma at least was not too unpleasant.

Moriarty and Nathan were inseparable. Nathan had even invested in a modest camper van, so that when he went on tour, or was away filming, they had a mobile home from home. This saved both the expense and unpleasantness of hotels and boarding houses. They escaped their unpredictable accommodation and lacklustre cuisine. It also gave them the freedom to enjoy each other's company undisturbed. The only drawback to this gypsy life was Moriarty's flatulence. A large dog can create an equally sized miasma.

Moriarty even accompanied Nathan to his performances. He sat quietly in the wings scrounging biscuits from the stage crew. He would sit up, and then give them the long stare. The head would cock slightly to one side, the ears would half raise in anticipation, and the mouth would slightly open. At the point when he had their undivided attention, he would lay down his ace, the raised right paw. It always tipped them into the 'aawwhh' moment, so named for the inevitable sound they would make, just as they passed over the treat he had now acquired. His relaxed, affable manner meant he was welcomed by even the most tyrannical of directors, and occasionally he got a walk on part. Those performances were, in his opinion, the stand out moment of any production.

Just before 12 noon and almost finished with the crossword, Nathan ambled across the worn stone flags to the bar. Moriarty watched him intently. Ears cocked, trying to look nonchalant, while actually eavesdropping with all his powers of concentration. Although deprived of a time piece, his familiarity with their routine meant that he knew that this was the pivotal moment of the day: the lunch order was about to be placed. Most dog owners will at some point say 'I swear he understands every word I say.' In Moriarty's case this really was true. Like all wolfhounds he had an extensive and impressive vocabulary, he just sometimes pretended to be hard of understanding, particularly when asked to do something he considered unwelcome, or beneath his dignity. Today he waited for the words, 'pie' or 'fish.' He knew it would be one or the other, it all depended on the whim of his friend with the opposable thumbs and wallet. Since both came with chips, he would be happy either way, but if pressed to choose, his preference would always be for 'pie.' Today to his delight the word 'pie' floated back, and the inevitable salivation process started.

Returning to his table, Nathan spent the next few minutes finishing the crossword. It was a good day today, he only had three clues unanswered. After some thought he had filled those gaps with 'nascent', 'malleable' and 'custard.' As often happened his mind went slightly sideways, and the thought passed through his consciousness that when you considered it, every nascent custard was by nature malleable. As he entered the last letter of the final word, lunch arrived. The next few minutes were passed in happy consumption. Moriarty was fed chips one at a time from Nathan's hand. It always surprised onlookers at the dainty way he would take the food from Nathan's fingers. Teeth that looked capable of biting through steel cables gently and dexterously removed one chip after another. Sections of shortcrust pastry with a hint of gravy were also likewise devoured.

Washing everything down with the remains of his ale, Nathan procured the next pint and sat back down. Picking up his copy of The Stage he began to idly flick through it. When he reached the section devoted to upcoming auditions his life was turned upside down. He carefully put the pint down. It was clear he would need both hands to hold the magazine as his fingers were shaking. He read it again. Then went through it a third time. What he had just read changed his entire world. The pub faded out of conscious view. He was eleven years old again. One Sunday afternoon, replete with that most middle class suburban lunch (the English roast) he saw "Lawrence of Arabia" for the very first time. He was spellbound. That moment was for him a "Road to Damascus." From then on, his sole aim in life was to be an actor. No, not just an actor. He wanted to be Peter O'Toole. He had never seen anyone dominate a scene like that. When O'Toole was on screen, he was the focal point, no-one else mattered. Nathan wanted that same sheer, vital, dynamic presence; he wanted every eye to be on him.

In the years that followed he devoured every recording he could get his hands on. Every possible example of O'Toole's work was acquired. It became an obsession. DVDs and videos were played repeatedly. Notebooks were filled with a dissection of dialogue, intonation, pausing, sense stress, movement, body language and gestures. Hours were spent in his bedroom practising every little thing that made O'Toole, O'Toole. Later in life, despite his parents' misgivings, he pursued his chosen career of 'Actor.' Securing a place at RADA, he strode in the footsteps of his idol, his eyes fixed on the goal of being the most O'Toole actor possible. Getting parts as an extra were pursued and then achieved. The first speaking parts came along, even if they were only one line. Now, he was a moderately successful actor; but somehow along the way, the years had made the spark disappear. He was now financially content, he enjoyed his work and the people he worked with, but he had lost his fire. His goal had disappeared from view. He had become comfortable, complacent and rudderless.

In this one heart stopping moment, everything had changed. Sitting in the dim shadows of the Lord Nelson, his entire world stopped turning. It hung suspended for a moment of infinite time. On the page in front of him was the announcement that within a year, auditions would begin for the film "Rogue Male." The aim was to select the lead actor for what was to be a biopic of the life of Peter O'Toole. They were looking for the perfect actor to bring to life the story of that great man. For the first time in years, he felt truly alive, energised. He had to get that part. He became an actor because of that man. He was born to be Peter O'Toole. He had the height. He had the look. He could even do the voice. This was the perfect point for him to do it. At this age with the right makeup and lighting he could play both the younger and older O'Toole.

The only real obstacle that he could see was that he needed to be far more successful than he was right now. The production of this movie would cost millions of dollars. At this precise moment in time, he was the casting director's view of a 'nobody.' He needed to become a 'somebody,' and he had only twelve months to do it in. He needed a plan. This was his destiny.

Laying the paper down he drained the pint and collected Moriarty's lead. This confused Moriarty somewhat as the normal routine included one more pint and he was therefore daydreaming, considering which doorways or posts he would leave his particular fragrant calling card on when they gently ambled home. Nathan returned his empty glass to the bar. Eric, the equally confused barman, was halfway through pulling the expected third pint. He stopped mid-pull. Brows furrowed.

'You going Mr Stockwood?'

Nathan stood shoulders back, spine stiff and confident. His eyes shone with a new passion and determination. He smiled at the bemused Eric.

'Needs must dear boy, my destiny is beckoning.'

'Destiny?' queried the frowning barman.

Nathan paused as a new thought rose clearly and quite obviously in his mind.

'On the other hand, the thing about destiny is that it is, well, for want of a better word, destined. Continue with the pint and add to it a double Laphroaig and a packet of salt and vinegar crisps for the faithful hound. Destiny should always be celebrated.'

Moriarty, while momentarily nonplussed at the prospect of leaving early, was relieved to walk back to their table, while Nathan carried the tray of liquid and culinary delights. Moriarty relaxed again, particularly as his immediate future now unexpectedly involved crisps, an unanticipated bonus to the day. Wolfhounds, while great thinkers and philosophers, are first and foremost pragmatists. And whichever way you look at it, one should never look a gift crisp in the packet.

So, the two companions drank, ate, and drew up their plans.

2

THE RAINBOW THIEF

It was much later than usual when Nathan finally departed the Lord Nelson and commenced his joyous, if somewhat uncoordinated way home. His destination was the ground floor apartment of a converted, clifftop Georgian town house. This he had bought fifteen years before on the proceeds acquired by playing a recurring character in a police procedural drama series. He had inhabited the role of the rookie Detective Constable, who with his naivety and innocence, provided the only light relief in an otherwise grim tale of death and suffering. His late exit from the pub was due to the intensive plotting and planning he had been engrossed in.

Although it was a walk of only a few minutes, Nathan had adopted a studied approach to this journey. He was employing the precise, careful walk of a man who is very well aware that he is just a touch tipsy, and yet does not want anyone else to know it. As a result, he was walking somewhat slower than usual. Fortunately, Moriarty had seen this before, though very rarely, as his friend was not, unlike the celebrated O'Toole, a heavy drinker. Male wolfhounds, as a breed, are a particularly gregarious bunch, and they enjoy spreading their unique scent on every lamppost, door frame and gate. After all something this special should be shared. Today however, he realised that particular pleasure, and in fact duty, would have to be foregone. It would need all his steadying weight, and substantial bulk to keep Nathan both upright and on the pavement.

Nathan progressed with the loose, graceful, floating walk of the totally relaxed man. His stride was long, unhurried and fluid. Only in the last inch of each stride was there the briefest pause, as he checked exactly where the floor was. Moriarty ambled alongside, his substantial chest wedged against Nathan's hip, serving as both support and guide. Thus, man and dog literally, and emotionally joined at the hip, made their unsteady and slightly laborious way home.

Getting to his apartment Nathan stood before the door. He swayed back and forth as though in a high wind, while he rummaged through a succession of pockets in search of his keys. He eventually found them on the third lap of his clothing; they were in the pocket he had started with. The next challenge was unlocking the door. Bending down induced a minor dizzy spell and tipping forward, he bounced his head smartly off the door panel. Taking two rapid steps backwards he regained his equilibrium. He attempted the task of lining up the key with the hole for a second time. His brow furrowed as he approached the test with the focused, careful, steady precision of a man tasked with disarming the thermonuclear device at the end of the film with only five seconds on the clock.

Successfully opening the door, he strode in. His attempt to keep the illusion of sobriety was spoilt only by his tripping over the entrance mat and measuring his length on the floor. Instantly springing up, he almost shot straight backwards out of the door. Moriarty's head was inserted smartly between his buttocks, and then shoved forward to keep him upright. Tossing his keys on the small table in the hall and missing, he stepped briskly, if erratically through the apartment to open the French doors leading out onto the terrace overlooking the sea. This was a prerequisite, as every wolfhound owner will tell you. In any building the exterior doors must always be open, or complaints will follow. Your wolfhound always needs a minimum of at least one exterior door open at any given point in time, just in case he wants to go out, or maybe just to lay down in front of and consider his domain through the open portal. If the door is shut the Wolfhound will invariably be on the wrong side of it, and you will have to open it to let him in. Of course, after your hound has entered woe betide you if you think you can then shut the door behind them.

Dropping gratefully into a deeply upholstered leather chair with a sigh and a tiny suppressed belch, Nathan reached for the telephone. All the calls he made were from a landline. He had a Luddite distaste for many of the trappings of modern life and eschewed the possession of a mobile phone, smart or otherwise. Now it was time to set the wheels of his plan in motion. He needed to call his agent.

Trelawney Mancroft, Theatrical Agent, sat at his antique office desk with his head in his hands. His elbows were propped on the vast, varnished wooden top. His substantial stomach (only just encased in a mustard-coloured waistcoat), was uncomfortably pressed into the edge. He sighed deeply.

He hated actors. A more self-indulgent, self-obsessed crowd of narcissistic, whining, neurotic, spoilt children it would be hard to imagine. Why did he do this to himself? What on earth had persuaded him to choose this career? He could have been something far less stressful like a test pilot or bomb disposal expert. Why Theatrical Agent? He must have been out of his tiny mind.

It was with these depressing and negative thoughts spiraling through his synapses that the phone rang. Upon answering he heard the purring, slurring voice of Nathan Stockwood. Despite his inner feelings, he replied with professional grace in an upbeat voice.

'Nathan my dear old chap, how wonderful to hear from you.'

'Trew, darling chum, I need to see you as soon as possible. I have a destiny. Are you free tomorrow?'

Trelawney paused.

'Let me see, just wait a moment.'

Pressing the mute button he gave vent to his feelings on actors, their parentage, and in particular, Nathan and his destiny. This took some time as he had quite a lot of feelings on the subject, and gave further weight to what he had already been thinking. It was an undeniable truth he thought, that all actors were fundamentally insane. Suppressing a groan of despair, he unmuted the phone.

'How about two o 'clock? My office?'

'Excellent. Polish up your little grey cells and get your book of contacts out. There is a part I want to get. No, a part I must get. It's the role I was born to play. O'Toole. They are making a film of his life. I am O'Toole. No one else can play this part. It's mine. I want it. To get it I need to be a star, and we only have twelve months to make me one.'

'A star? Well, if you say so old chap. You know I would do anything for my favourite client. I will see you tomorrow.'

Hanging up he sat back in his chair and ran his fingers through what was left of his hair and sighed deeply. The look on his face was reminiscent of a vulture who has just seen his lunch get back up and wander off. This was all he needed. Nathan Stockwood had now suddenly developed ambition. In the normal course of events directors and studios phoned him and asked specifically for Nathan. He never had to chase parts for him, or book him into auditions. Nathan Stockwood was regular money in the bank. A steady source of income without any of the unpleasantness of schmoozing for the work. People in the business knew Nathan, and his reliability to provide what they needed when they needed it. They even welcomed that oversized pungent hearth rug on legs that went everywhere with him. But now this perfect client had developed a destiny. It was all so unfair. Trelawney stared out of his window across the pitched peaks of the awnings of Norwich market and wondered what the world was coming to. One thing was certain, life definitely had it in for him.

One hour later, Nathan awoke with a startled jerk. He had not meant to fall asleep, but the combination of alcohol, and the excitement of the concept of his destiny had tired him. His mouth was bone dry and felt caked with something that had apparently been scraped from the bottom of a parrot's cage. If asked, Moriarty could have told him it was the combination of too much drink, and then falling asleep with your mouth open, but as ever his opinion was not sought. Rubbing his eyes Nathan tottered to the kitchen in search of refreshment. Armed with a tray containing a pot of extra strong tea, and a restorative packet of digestive biscuits he returned to the chair. Placing the tray on the small table next to him he surveyed his extensive collection of DVDs. Ninety percent of this was devoted to the works of Mr O'Toole. It was time to dive in and immerse himself in the work of the master. From this point onward he needed to live, breathe, eat, sleep, drink and think exactly like his mentor, his muse. Nothing less than total effort would be needed.

3

WHAT'S NEW PUSSY CAT

Nathan parked the van in one of the narrow side streets in the centre of the city. Norwich is what might be described as an economy sized city. It has few of the problems of the larger modern metropolis. Its dimensions, and indeed its architecture is firmly rooted in a bygone age. Centrally, you can walk almost anywhere in a relatively short time. For the car owner there were various official car parks, however the experienced local can find the little nooks and crannies that allow the free parking of, for example, a modest camper van.

He had wisely allowed more than double the required time for the short walk to his agent's office, as of course he had Moriarty with him. It was not that Moriarty was slow, far from it. The issue, living with a dog of this size, is that the owner must allow for the wow factor. People in general are not used to seeing a dog of such proportions. In fact, the only way one could attract more attention would be to walk through the streets with a tiger on a leash. Having a wolfhound with you meant that you never went anywhere very quickly. Almost every other person would stop you. All wolfhounds take it for granted that they are star material, and that the entire world revolves around them. Nathan on the other hand enjoyed the anonymity. Although a very recognisable face on stage and screen, when he was with Moriarty, he was invisible.

The Mancroft Theatrical Agency was located above a trendy scented candle store on the edge of Norwich market. Nathan and Moriarty made their way up the ancient tilted wooden stairs, Nathan at the rear, Moriarty in the lead. You don't want to be in front of a wolfhound on the stairs. As a general rule they don't really like stairs. They tend to take them at a bit of a rush. Behind is safer. It is also wise to let go of the lead. The alternative is the very real risk of shoulder joint dislocation.

As he climbed the stairs behind Moriarty's lumbering ascent, Nathan felt a shiver run through him. The night before he had spent hours watching O'Toole's films. After many years of toddling along as a competent jobbing actor he had once again immersed himself in those stunning performances. Alongside the rigor, just at the edge of conscious awareness, there was the faint sound of a voice. A voice he knew better than his own.

'On with the motley.'

The pure cut glass vowels of O'Toole had just trickled into his sub-conscious.

At the top of the stairs Moriarty turned and looked back at Nathan. Something was different. The only trouble was he could not quite work out what it was that had changed. something however was very definitely different. He could not be sure but Nathan seemed that little bit taller. His cheekbones were slightly more defined, and he was decidedly more confident.

Entering the suite of offices Nathan was struck by the misaligned look of the place. The building was partly Tudor. That plus its age meant it only had a nodding acquaintance with the concept of a right angle. The ceiling was low and ancient, yet the reception itself was decorated with the latest up to date 21st century office furniture. The glass and chrome looked oddly incongruous in the cramped Tudor room. They crossed the sloping plush carpeted floor to the sleek and shiny reception desk, seated behind which was Trelawney Mancroft's new slim and polished PA and receptionist, Ms Roots. She eyed them with some trepidation. Actors she was used to, but not when accompanied by large untidy hounds.

Moriarty sat and looked about, just in case there was a lost biscuit that was in need of rescue. Nathan leant over the desk and gave her a deeply captivating look. His eyes unblinking, a half-smile on his face he said in a deep, slow aristocratic voice.

'Good afternoon, Pussycat, we are here to see Trelawney.'

With hindsight it was perhaps unfortunate that the last O'Toole film he had watched before setting out was the 1965 comedy "What's New Pussycat." He was therefore deeply in the character of Michael Voltaire James. Sadly, it was a character that displayed the personality of a man who is somewhat offensive to the virtue signalling mind of modern youth. This has led many modern television stations to preface such films with the warning that the following programme "contains views and attitudes of its time." To be honest some of the attitudes of the main character of this particular film were probably questionable even in its time. O'Toole had played a man who was both irresistible to attractive women, and who could not himself resist beautiful women, and now Nathan was playing just such a man.

At any other time being called 'Pussycat' would have set Ms Roots into a fury of righteous feminist indignation. However, Nathan, tall, impeccably dressed, handsome and with the most intense blue eyes she had ever seen, momentarily blindsided her. As he stood there exuding the very essence of O'Toole she was mesmerised. She looked back in a state of slight shock. The languid smooth voice was like liquid chocolate. The stare from his eyes seemed to look into her very soul. Unable to look away from that magnetic gaze her fingers fumbled for the intercom.

'Mr Mancroft, there is a gentleman here to see you. With an enormous dog.'

'That will be Nathan, send them in.'

'You can go in now,' she said unnecessarily.

Once again, those eyes seemed to pin her to the chair. Slowly blinking he breathed a well-mannered reply.

'Thank you so much, you have been an absolute angel. Pussycat.'

As he and the large hound padded through the doorway into Mancroft's office, she suddenly became aware her mouth was hanging open. She shut it with a snap. What was wrong with her she fumed. She was a modern career woman. Who did he think he was? Calling her 'Pussycat.' A blush crept across her face. I simpered, she thought. I actually simpered. I have never simpered in my life. No one simpers anymore. It went out of fashion with fainting and having a fit of the vapours. I've just singlehandedly put women's rights back fifty years.

The furnishings of Trelawney's office were the polar opposite of the reception. It seemed more akin to a Victorian gentleman's club than a modern work environment. It was all leather and wood panelling, with an enormous antique desk which dominated the room. Behind it, like a modern-day Mr Pickwick, the short rotund form of Trelawney Mancroft seemed somehow small and incongruous. Nathan draped himself comfortably in the leather wingback chair opposite the vast desk. Moriarty carried out a survey of the room just in case the lost biscuit was there. He even put his head in the waste bin and rooted around for a while; after all you never know. His search fruitless, he settled next to Nathan in his patented canine Sphinx pose. Although disappointed with the absence of anything edible, he nonetheless summoned up his patience and settled in to wait.

Nathan launched into the description of his destiny. Impassioned, vibrant and burning with his naked hunger for securing this one holy grail. The part he must have.

Trelawney listened patiently, and when the enthused actor finally paused to draw breath, made the first move in the plan he had spent half the night working out. His hope was to derail this absurdly ambitious project.

'My dear boy I entirely sympathise but it simply can't be done in the time allotted. Right now, you are a very bankable performer. You have an almost permanent demand for your services, you are in your niche. In your element. A square peg in a square hole. It would be impossible to propel you into stardom in the given time frame. You would need to be offered a starring part right now. That would need the most unlikely piece of luck.'

Nathan remained resolute.

'It must be done,' he insisted. 'I was born to play this role. I became an actor because of that man. No other actor can do this the way I will.'

Trelawney now played his winning hand. The solution that was so crazy even an obsessed hare-brained actor would not countenance it.

'Look, the only way you could possibly do it is by replacing the lead in your current show. You have just done the initial two month run out in the provinces in that farce comedy thing haven't you? What is it called again?'

"Always Listen to Mother Girls." It's a sub-Wodehouse comedy set in a country home full of posh people. Yes, we are currently on a short break before hitting the bigger town and city theatres for two months. We start in Cambridge, go up the eastern side of the country, make a brief foray into Scotland then come back down the western side finishing in Oxford, before a final month in the West End. The first two months were to get any wrinkles out of the performance.'

'Right' said Trelawney. 'Then all you have to do is nobble the leading man.'

Nathan sat for a moment completely stunned. He shouted, 'are you crazy? What possible use would that be?'

'Hear me out' pleaded Trelawney, raising a placatory hand. 'Look, you know what these touring theatre productions are like. It's called show business, but the emphasis is all on the business not on the show, and touring is a very expensive undertaking. There isn't any spare cash for separate understudies. You all understudy the part of the actor above you on the billing. Take the leading man out of the equation, and you step into his shoes. The local critics in the bigger venues will review your magnificent last-minute stand in performance, and good reviews will build up a head of steam and enthusiasm for your exceptional acting talents. By the time you get to the West End, the London critics will lap it up. Then, and only then can I get you bigger, better parts. Starring parts. Put simply, the only thing that will sway casting directors to give you those starring parts is for you to be a smash hit as a star with critics and audiences. To get star parts you have to be a star in the first place.'

He leaned forward resting his elbows on the desk, and steepling his fingers placed his chin on the tips. Got him he thought, only a complete lunatic would even consider such a crazy, criminal course of action. He watched Nathan carefully. The actor looked as though someone had just kicked him in the stomach. Deflated, defeated and brought to earth with a bump by the mother of all reality checks.

Then he straightened up, gripped the arms of the chair and with his face glowing with renewed fervour he declared,

'Brilliant. I knew you would come through for me. Genius. It cannot fail. We go back on tour tomorrow and I will follow your advice to the letter. Nobble old Lancelot, stuffy old ham. He won't know what has hit him.'

Trelawney twitched in shock, his elbows slid off the desk, and he came within a whisker of cracking his jaw on the desk top.

'No. Really no, you can't.'

'Oh yes, I can. It's destiny. It's your idea, and it's a good one.' Leaping to his feet he grabbed his agent's limp hand and pumped it up and down with excessive vigour. 'Genius, absolute genius.' Giving Trelawney a final mighty slap on the shoulder, he bounded from the office, Moriarty in his wake.

As they strode out into the outer reception Ms Roots eyed them suspiciously. This time she was ready for him. There would be no simpering. Nathan turned his face to her and this time he gave her the full thousand-watt smile, the eyes cobalt blue and intense. He stepped over to her, lifted her right hand, and gently brushed his lips against her knuckles.

'Thank you so much, you are magnificent. Pussycat.'

Dropping her hand they exited, Moriarty in the lead.

As dangerous as it is to be in front of wolfhounds going up a flight of stairs, it is downright suicidal to be in front of them going down. They don't so much descend, as carry out a sort of controlled avalanche.

Back in the reception Ms Roots sat stunned as the sound of their departure rattled up the stairway: a cacophonous noise reminiscent of a workman dropping a tea chest full of horseshoes down a cobbled road.

With a start she realised she could hear a distant voice yelling. Sadly, the voice she could hear was her own, screaming from deep within her mind as her enraged inner feminist shouted.

'Traitor, you not only simpered, this time you giggled.'

4

HOW TO STEAL A MILLION

Moriarty and Nathan ambled gently back to the van. Such was his preoccupation that even the enthusiastic questioning of passers-by about Moriarty failed to register on his conscious mind. He just shambled past in a zombie like trance. How? He thought. That was the big question. How? Lancelot Sigismund DeVere, LSD to those who knew him (so named as any amount of time spent in his company was likely to warp your view of reality), was the writer, producer, director and leading actor of the Kemp Players. He wasn't the greatest actor in the world, but he was certainly in the top ten biggest egos in the acting profession. LSD didn't just see himself as an actor or performer, no, he was an impresario from a bygone age. He was the Herbert Beerbohm Tree of the modern world. He had to dominate any gathering of his fellow actors. They must all become planets that orbited his bright star.

Nathan had to find a way to replace him in this production. However, it must be finely judged. He didn't want to cause the poor old chap any lasting harm, but he must get him out of the running, only then could Nathan step into his role as star of the show. After all they were friends of a kind. Well, they had worked together a lot. This would need some careful planning, meticulous working out. Climbing back into the van Nathan snapped shut the safety belt and started the engine. Moriarty sat just behind him resting his chin on Nathan's shoulder. This left the inevitable but growing patch of drool. Perhaps, mused Nathan, something would come to him if he slept on it.

Early the following morning, still with no clear idea of how to evict LSD from his position as star, the two companions got back in the van and headed for Cambridge. Today was the first day back with the company. They were due to meet in a community centre in the suburbs of Cambridge that morning. LSD wanted a read through of the play, followed by a full dress-rehearsal at the Cambridge Corn Exchange theatre in the afternoon. All of this just prior to their opening night that evening.

He parked in the bland anonymous car park of the community centre set in the middle of an unimaginative suburb, and headed for the front doors of the low bland building. It struck him that he had done this same thing so many times that it was now getting increasingly difficult to tell one community centre from another.

Enroute across the indifferently patched and weed riven tarmac studded with tufts of determined weeds, he met the first of his peers. Deidre Hintlesham was tall, slim and blonde. She was playing the American friend of the leading lady Jenny Lynd, and was Nathan's love interest in the play.

Warm greetings exchanged, they linked arms in friendly camaraderie and entered the open echoing space of the hall. Like all such establishments it was indifferently decorated in a wipeable paint that defied identification as to its actual colour. It was cold, over lit with fluorescent strips, and had a floor that insisted on producing a tooth grinding squeak with every step one took. Against one wall draped with wipeable oilcloth stood two cheap wooden trestle tables with an urn, an eclectic collection of disparate mugs, tea, coffee, milk, sugar and an assortment of biscuits. While the pair armed themselves with drinks and called out greetings to those of the cast that had arrived before them, Moriarty fixed the biscuit plate with a hard stare. He was too well brought up to just help himself, so by way of a gentle hint he stood on Jenny's foot. Having got her attention, he gave her his most appealing look. Reaching out she picked up a biscuit and Moriarty's heart beat just that little bit faster. She had chosen his favourite. LSD had laid on a magnificent spread consisting of a battered box of the cheapest teabags, a jar of slightly congealed instant coffee, plastic pots of long-life milk and a plate of biscuits from one of those selection boxes that is firmly rooted in the 1950's. Custard Creams, Bourbons and joy of joys Jammie Dodgers. While Moriarty would never reject any biscuit, for sheer value for money the Jammie Dodger outshone all its rivals. It was the Wolfhound Holy Grail of biscuits. The biscuit and cream sections dissolved quickly enough in his mouth, but the glutinous disc of jam was another matter. It was felt amongst those who knew and fed Moriarty that you hadn't really lived till you had watched him tackle one. It was a sight like no other. The extended chomping, slurping and concomitant drooling could, on occasions, exceed five minutes per biscuit.

Within a few minutes all the cast were assembled and chatting happily while cradling hot mugs in cold hands. Except the leading man was absent. Finally, with a reverberating crash as the doors closed behind him, Lancelot Sigismund DeVere made his entrance. Like all actors he had an irremovable streak of drama. As a result, when faced with double doors, his larger-than-life ego required he open both together, and stride through them with a flourish and suitable panache. Built along similar lines and of a similar age to Nathan he had however an extra layer of polish. His hair was perfectly arranged and his clothes were chosen with that fussy, extreme attention to detail that screamed 'Thespian.'

'Welcome my children, welcome. How wonderful to see you all. I have missed you all so very much.'

The cast members scattered and extracted plastic chairs from the stacks along the wall. Soon they were arranged in a circle with LSD at the head. It should be impossible to have a head to a circle, but he managed it. He principally achieved this by making sure there was a noticeably wider gap between his chair and those on either side of him. This carefully judged spacing both separated him from the pack, and marked him out as the Alpha in the gathering.

'I am so sorry to drag you all here but we must get it right tonight. Time to blow away the cobwebs and oil our rusting acting muscles, put our best foot forward and our shoulders to the wheel, our nose to the grindstone.' Having exhausted his current store of mixed metaphors he launched them into the opening scene of the script.

Sometime later, read through completed, the actors drifted away in search of a decent pub for lunch. Nathan and Lancelot stood and leant back against the edge of the hall stage, sipping hot tea.

Lancelot leaned in confidentially and whispered.

'You look well. The time off has obviously done you good. I just wish I could say the same. You have no idea what a terrible time I have had during the break. I swear I am a martyr to my digestive system. You would not believe the agonies I have had to endure. It's a wonder I am here at all.'

Nathan had completely forgotten that dear old LSD had a 'Stomach.' 'Stomach' in this instance meant that it was the centre of all his woes and troubles. It was at that moment the light bulb went on above Nathan's head. That was the answer as to how. An army marches on its stomach but he, Nathan Stockwood would march on Lancelot's stomach. All he needed to do was find a way to get LSD to rule himself out of the play on gastrointestinal grounds. The only trick was how to get Lancelot's stomach to bring him down. At this point he only had half an idea, now he needed to bring it into practical existence. Nathan and Moriarty left the van in the car park and walked in search of a suitable pub, preferably one without any of his fellow actors in it. He needed space to think of how to get LSD's stomach to play up on cue.

5

WINGS OF FAME

The answer as to how to put his plan into action was apparent in the very first moments of the dress rehearsal. He knew he needed to get Lancelot's stomach to act up on cue and make him so unwell he could not continue. This would allow him as lead understudy to step in. He also grasped that for this to happen he needed to have something suitably noxious for Lancelot to eat or drink either before, or early on in the performance. The answer was in the play's opening scene. Lancelot, playing Rodney Hetheringham, and the leading actress Jenny Lynd, playing Abigail Willoughby-Smyth, opened with a scene in which they lamented the opposition of her father, Colonel Willoughby-Smyth (Johnathon Hobvert) and her aunt Amelia (Penelope Blickwell) to their marriage. In the course of this scene Shaw the butler (Joseph Cripper) entered and served them two martinis complete with rubber olives on cocktail sticks. The martinis were simply water of course, but Nathan realised they were the perfect medium to introduce something toxic to make Lancelot, and only Lancelot very unwell.

The final question was what could he use to achieve his goal? After the rehearsals were finished, they had two hours before curtain up, and the cast scattered to get something to eat. Nathan however went with Moriarty in search of a pharmacy. He found one just a couple of streets away and looping Moriarty's lead over an adjacent bollard, he entered.

Approaching the girl behind the counter he whispered,

'This is a little delicate, but,' here he dropped his voice to an even lower tone, 'could you tell me what are the strongest over the counter laxatives you have in stock?'

The girl gave a little half smile and leaning forward gave him the requisite information. Nathan followed the advice and made the purchase. A few more minutes were spent walking, and Nathan unearthed a second pharmacy. This time he purchased another packet of a different brand of laxative from a counter assistant who was also suitably discreet and sympathetic. The third pharmacy took nearly twenty minutes to find, but once there he got yet another brand of a third different laxative to add to his collection.

He planned to leave nothing to chance. So, opening one capsule from each of the three packets, he decanted the internal powder into a clean envelope obtained from an adjacent Post Office. Giving the envelope a little shake to thoroughly mix its contents, he sealed it and slipped it into his jacket pocket. Although knowing very little of pharmaceuticals he reasoned three different powders mixed should be explosive in their effect. Grabbing a quick snack, he and Moriarty got back to the theatre a good hour before curtain up. This he reasoned should give him a clear run to the table in the wings where the various props for the performance were laid out. Going to the stage door, the doorman nodded him through. Extracting the biro from his mouth and laying aside his Sudoku, the grizzled doorman spoke with the rasping voice of a man who had honed his vocal cords on a lifetime of whisky and roll up cigarettes.

'You're a keen one. I've not seen any one else from your lot yet.'

Nathan muttered a brief reply,

'Oh, you know, first night nerves. I just thought I would sit in my dressing room for a bit before we start. Make myself a coffee. Get my thoughts together.'

He was convinced both his guilt, and every nuance of his plan was plainly written across his face. The doorman seemed unconcerned, he just grunted and turned his mind back to his puzzle book.

Ascending the dark narrow stairwell, he reached the back stage area. It was a dimly lit cavernous space. Layers of backdrops hung suspended above him like giant dusty bats waiting for the sun to set. More ropes and pulleys than could be found on a large schooner were secured in great looping arcs from the rear brick wall. Looming in the half-light, large clunky electrical lighting boards with banks of switches, sat looking like a steampunk version of the controls for the Tardis. Set stage right, just inside the wings, was the props table. Each item laid out in the order they would be needed by the actors as the play progressed. From left to right they were, one rubber chicken, two tennis racquets (wooden), a pile of books, a bowl of trifle, a tray with one whisky and soda (cold tea), a set of boxing gloves, a cricket bat and last but not least the very first props of the show, a tray with two martinis complete with rubber olives.

Nathan had watched very carefully during the rehearsal. Roughly halfway through the opening scene Shaw entered stage right bearing the tray. Jenny took the glass on Shaw's left, and Lancelot the one to the right. Thinking back, he was sure that was what he had seen every time they had played the scene in the previous two months. Tearing open the envelope he poured the contents into the glass destined for LSD. He gave it a quick stir with the rubber olive. The liquid swirled, and then dissolved the fine white powder, leaving it just as clear and innocent looking as its companion. He carefully placed it back in position on the tray. The envelope was folded and slipped discreetly into his pocket. Turning he headed for his dressing room; Moriarty padding dutifully behind him.

Nathan had provided himself with a kettle and a cafetiere in his dressing room, and now he fortified himself with caffeine as he changed into his opening costume, and applied his makeup. As he worked, the first sounds of his fellow actors arriving filtered through the closed door. Chattering, laughing and with clumping footsteps the sound of the cast members filled the backstage area. A little later, the faint muted buzz of the assembling audience excitedly talking drifted down to his room.

Ten minutes before curtain up he went out and installed himself stage left. This put him on the opposite side from the props table. He wanted to be sure he was nowhere near the props just in case any suspicion should fall on him. He felt jumpy and twitchy, and found it almost impossible to stand still. It surprised him just how nervous all this had made him. Moriarty, standing alongside, looked up at him. He knew his friend was worried but had no idea why.

The orchestra struck up the opening music, the auditorium lights went down, and the curtain parted as the stage lights went up. Standing centre stage was Lancelot, debonair and dignified in spats, slacks, blazer and cravat, a fake cigarette in an elegant holder. Jenny facing him was svelte and stylish in a silky flapper dress. The play began.

The scene seemed to unreel with a treacle like slowness to Nathan as he nervously waited for Shaw's entrance. Shaw however was a long way from nervous. In fact, by contrast he had missed his call and was still in his dressing room. His attention was fixed on the results of a horse race. He had placed a substantial bet on a very well tipped horse. His eyes were glued to his smart phone, checking the internet to see if his hopes had been fulfilled, and that he was richer at a rate of ten to one. A frantic stage manager burst into his room.

'What are you doing, you are supposed to be on in less than two minutes.'

Shaw sprinted out of the room, his 'sorry' floating back behind him. Getting stage right just as he heard his cue, he grabbed the tray. He cantered over to the edge of the wings. His momentum caused both glasses to skid violently across the tray. Recovering his balance and the glasses by the merest whisker. Drawing himself up into his best butler stance, he paused for a brief moment to realign the glasses, then strode with a ponderous, stately grace onto the stage. Lancelot, with his back to the audience, gave him a withering glower.

Blast the man he thought. He is getting to be the giddy limit. That's the third time he has almost missed his cue since we started this run. He made a mental note to have some serious words with him. Turning back to his leading lady he smiled, and on they went with the scene. Jenny at least, he thought was the consummate professional.

Nathan breathed out for what seemed the first time in ten minutes. Yes. Stage one complete, now to settle back and wait for the resulting explosion.

Nathan was not sure how long the powder would need to take effect, and the strain of waiting made him edgy and distracted. Even he realised his performance tonight was off. He could feel his fellow actors mentally frowning at him. Just after the interval they were midway through a scene with most of the cast all on stage at the same time. Nathan found he could not take his eyes off Lancelot. The suspense was killing him. Jenny, the only major cast member not on stage made her entrance on cue from stage left. On her third step she visibly faltered, almost stumbling. Recovering, she pinned the smile back on her face, and took a deep breath for her line. Instead of her dialogue she emitted the strangest gurgling sound. She stopped. Her mouth opened again, and still no words came out. The colour drained from her face. Beads of sweat suddenly appeared on her forehead. Her eyes opening wide in shock, she pressed a hand to her stomach as an even louder and more liquid gurgle erupted. This time even the audience could hear it. To her credit she drew herself up and tried the line again, but nothing came out except a small squeak then a groan from deep within her. Clutching her stomach, she turned and sprinted for the wings. Nathan felt horror grip him like a cold clammy hand on the back of his neck. Oh no, oh no, that twit of a butler, Shaw had switched the glasses.

Even in his state of stunned shock, Nathan was impressed by the speed Jenny was travelling at. It was amazing just how fast she could run in high heels and a tight skirt. From Jenny's point of view the speed was not at all surprising. She was convinced that her goal of reaching the backstage toilet was in danger of not being achieved. While she felt sure she would get there, she was far less sanguine that the contents of her bowel would still be with her when she arrived. Abandoning the race for the toilet she veered for the closer sanctuary of the nearby cleaning cupboard, pausing only to grab a waist high ceramic Chinese vase left over from last year's panto. Hurling herself inside she slammed the door.

Back on stage the assembled cast gaped in shock. Lancelot took charge. Turning to the audience he broke the fourth wall.

'I am terribly sorry ladies and gentleman there will be brief delay in our play. Please accept our apologies. We won't be long.'

Waving to the stage manager he hissed 'curtain, curtain.'

The entire cast followed him out shuffling through the wings. Looking round he realised he had no idea where Jenny had gone. The lighting man standing with his mouth open in stunned surprise, pointed dumbly at the cleaning cupboard. Lancelot knocked timorously on the door. The cast huddled behind him.

'Jenny, Jenny darling. Are you in there?'

A voice that sounded nothing like Jenny's echoed back through the door.

'Go away, don't come in, just go away.'

The next sound to come out was not a voice. It was in fact, impossible to describe. The major drawback to using a large ceramic vase as a makeshift, well, shall we say, receptacle, is the echo factor. Suffice to say the sheer unpleasantness of the noises coming from the cupboard were enough to make the entire cast take several steps back. It wasn't just the sounds themselves so much as the length of time they went on for. The noise just kept on going. Added to which it was punctuated by piteous groans from Jenny. Frankly, it chilled the blood. Nathan found himself wracked with guilt. Nobbling a pompous oaf like LSD was one thing, but poisoning an old friend and fellow actor whom he rather liked was another thing altogether.

After several minutes the door to the cupboard inched slowly open and a pale shadow of Miss Jenny Lynd appeared. Clutching the door frame for support she attempted a brave though somewhat pale and sweaty smile.

'It's all right, just give me a moment and I will be OK.'

There was a long pause as the cast took in her trembling, somewhat disarrayed appearance. A loud gurgle broke the silence. Her eyes opened wide in horror.

'Oh no, please, no more. Not again.'

The door slammed shut. This time with a finality they all could recognise.

Lancelot swallowed and declared,

'Right, you all know the drill, we've prepared for this: understudies into costume, the show must go on.'

Nathan stood quietly absorbing the full awfulness of what he had just done. Destiny nil, Lancelot one. Moriarty on the other hand watched contentedly. In his opinion this play had just got a lot more entertaining.

6

THE FINAL CURTAIN

Nathan was already awake when the sun filtered in through the thin curtains of the van. He had not slept well. His dreams had been haunted by memories of the sounds that had echoed and reverberated from the small cleaning cupboard backstage. He had at first found it difficult to drop off. Then when he did succumb to the arms of Morpheus, he constantly jerked awake as his subconscious kept running the movie of his actions over and over again.

Throughout his life he had always considered himself to be quite a pleasant, affable, considerate man. He had gone along very happily and serenely. He had tried to never deliberately upset or hurt anyone. "Hail fellow and well met" was his motto. But now he had just poisoned an innocent woman, a peer. An actor he really liked, and considered a friend. And so, the bright sunny morning found him stretched out in his bed, hands behind his head staring at the ceiling, fretting and brooding on a side of his personality he now decided he didn't like very much. A fatigue headache buzzed and nipped at the inside of his forehead, with a sensation akin to a determined group of tiny miners trying to drill their way out.

Somewhat to his shame, he was now having mixed emotions about the whole affair. On the one hand was the guilt. He kept hearing the appalling noises echoing out of that cupboard. It was a ghastly experience; one he was in no hurry to repeat. It was like standing outside a cell listening to the Spanish Inquisition going to work. He was deeply upset having seen the strained, white, sweaty face of a woman who had just passed through such a harrowing ordeal. On the other hand, he was quite pleased with the efficacy of his plan. He felt a flush of success and accomplishment. He had been both surprised and impressed with the three-powder potion, which certainly had spectacular results. He just needed to get the right target.

So began the process all humans are capable of. Rationalisation. He had just committed an act that was at best morally dubious, and he was considering doing it again. Only this time to the correct target. All of us go through life with ourselves cast in the role of hero. It was other people who were the villains in the story, not us. Nathan was no different. Everything he did, even the dubious, less salubrious things, had to have a good reason behind them. So, he had to square it with his conscience. In this case that meant that his ambition picked his conscience up by the scruff of the neck, and put it in a sound proof box, then locked it away deep in the recesses of his mind.

After all he told himself there was no real harm done here. It was a fact of life that we all go to the toilet every day. It was nature's way of reminding us of our mortality, of our all too solid flesh. All he had done was condense Jenny's daily visits into one rather prolonged one. Yes, you could say that in one sense he had done a bad thing, but he had done it in a good cause. That part must be his. It would be short changing the writers and makers of the film, and even the public, of something wonderful if he allowed someone else to play Peter O'Toole. Didn't people say, "you can't make an omelette without breaking eggs," or "the end justifies the means." If you looked at it the right way he was acting (no pun intended) for the greater good. In fact, if you really thought about it long enough, it wasn't even his fault. If Joseph Cripper hadn't been late for his cue and rushed his entrance, the drinks would never have been misaligned on the tray and swapped round. You could even fairly legitimately say that it was Joseph who poisoned Jenny, and not him. It wasn't actually his fault Jenny was poisoned. Lancelot was the real target, and he had to be taken out of the running. He already suffered with his 'stomach.' A good purgative might, in the long run, actually do him some good. Early childhood memories of his mother surfaced, dessert spoon in hand, pouring castor oil into his protesting mouth. Her litany of 'now don't be silly, open wide this will do you a world of good' echoed from the mists of time.

Having successfully dealt with his conscience and inner qualms, he breathed a satisfied sigh. In reality his conscience had by now given up protesting, and was now sulking in the box, awaiting its chance to escape and get its own back. Feeling more sanguine about it all, a weary, slightly sweaty Nathan unstuck himself from the clammy sheets, and tottered weakly to the kitchen for restorative tea. Moriarty by contrast had slept the sleep of the righteous. Stretched out on the sofa he had no guilt, no remorse, just dreams of chasing biscuits. Hearing Nathan moving about, Moriarty shifted position just enough to raise one paw and receive his morning tummy rub. This ritual was a permanent part of their morning routine. If he was scratched in just the right spot, the one he couldn't quite reach himself, his back legs did a more than passable impression of a wolfhound riding an invisible bike.

Nathan and Moriarty arrived at the theatre at half nine. Due to Jenny's unexpected illness, Lancelot had told the cast the night before that there would be an emergency rehearsal at ten that morning. This was to allow the understudies to get properly up to speed with their new roles. Lancelot had chosen to get them to meet at the theatre, and rehearse on the stage, so in addition to reading the script, they could physically walk through each scene. Any live performance was as much about the movements on the stage as the spoken dialogue. Hence the old acting adage of making sure you "remember your lines and don't bump into the furniture."

The cast were in a subdued mood as they assembled at the theatre. The shocking events of the previous night's performance had left them all a little shaken. In addition, half of them had spent a large part of the night preparing for their unexpected understudy roles. Lancelot called them to order.

'You will all be pleased to know that Jenny is doing well. Not surprisingly she is rather shaken up after last night's events, and the doctor has recommended she take at least forty-eight hours off to get her feet back under her. So, for the duration of the Cambridge run Deidre will fill in for her, and all the younger female cast members will move up one to take the roles they have been understudying. You Penny will of course continue as Aunt Agatha. Lovely as you are darling, you can't play a character who is nineteen years old. That means everyone goes up one, and Rachel our second assistant stage manager will step in as the Maid. Don't worry love it's a non-speaking part and you only have a couple of scenes. Jenny will be back with us in three days just in time for us to start the Peterborough run.'

Deidre nodded sagely. A true professional, she was more than ready to step up one in the billing. Rachel looked nervous, her sudden step up to actually being on stage was a first for her. Penny however was pinched lipped and frowning, no woman likes to be told she can't play nineteen, even when she is fifty-five.

Nathan made a decision right there and then that he would hold fire on his next attempt. To have Lancelot fall ill with the very same problem as Jenny had just displayed the night before, would arouse suspicions. Better wait till they hit Peterborough. His problem was how to deliver the pellet with the poison? He could not repeat the spiking of the martinis. Last night had proved it was all too prone to human error. No, he needed a fool-proof delivery system. The flagon with the dragon or the vessel with the pestle? Which would have the pellet with the poison, and which would hold the brew that was true?

As they went through the play, scene by scene, the answer once again presented itself to him. Just before the interval there was a scene in which Lancelot, and only Lancelot drank a faux whisky and soda. There could be no chance of a mix up. It was impossible for someone else to be poisoned.

Lancelot would be on stage with Penny Blickwell as Aunt Amelia, and Johnathon Hobvert playing Colonel Willoughby-Smyth. Joseph, as the butler, would be to one side holding the tray with the whisky. At the mid-point in the scene, Lancelot was supposed to stride to the front of the stage, make his ultimatum to Amelia and the Colonel about getting married to Abigail, then he would turn round, walk over to Shaw the butler, grab the whisky, and down it in one, then slam the glass back on the tray with a flourish of defiance.

Nathan and Deidre in this scene were due to enter stage left fresh from the tennis court. They were to be attired in the obligatory tennis whites, it being a staple of all such comedies that someone at some point always enters so dressed. This is known universally in the trade as the "anyone for tennis" moment. This trope was not seen as often these days, but Lancelot as author of this play was firmly rooted in the 1930's. Nathan thought back to the previous night, calculating the time it took from when Jenny drank the potion, to the onset of her symptoms, and her rapid exit. Yes, it should work. Even factoring in Lancelot's greater physical bulk, he should start to feel the effects just before the final scene. Take him out then, and Nathan would be forced to step-in and play the last scene, just in time for the final curtain. Thereby he would single-handedly save the play and receive the applause and plaudits of cast and audience alike. Judging by the effect on Deidre, Lancelot should be out of action for days, especially when you took into account his fixation on the troubles of his 'stomach.' His already phobic obsession on his internal plumbing would hopefully tip him over the edge, and make him back off from playing the lead role for the whole tour, especially if Nathan could put in a bravura performance. The combination of good reviews, sold out performances, and his own gastric frailty would hopefully do the trick. Now he had a workable plan of action clear in his mind, Nathan relaxed. He just had to wait for the start of the Peterborough run and then he could swing into action. The game was afoot.

7

BRIGHT YOUNG THINGS

Opening night at the New Theatre, Peterborough:

His first attempt at poisoning Lancelot had been successful, with the exception of missing his target and inflicting collateral damage to the innocent Jenny. At least from an operational point of view it had worked. So, he thought it prudent to put exactly the same tactics into action for his second attempt.

Stage one: he arrived a good hour before curtain up. Strolling with nonchalant calm in through the stage door, with Moriarty in close attendance.

Stage two: get past the stage doorman. Once again, a small grizzled man of indeterminate age. He was almost identical to his counterpart in Cambridge, (Nathan wondered for a moment if perhaps stage doormen were cloned in some secret theatrical laboratory). The weather-beaten face looked up at him quizzically. The same question was asked, with the same whisky and tobacco voice.

'You're a keen one, not seen any one else from your lot yet.'

The same answer allayed any suspicions.

'Oh, you know, first night nerves. Just thought I would sit in my dressing room, make myself a coffee, and get my thoughts together.'

Satisfied, the doorman nodded and returned to his puzzle book. Not sudoku this time but a copy of "Where's Wally." Still, it takes all sorts, thought Nathan.

Stage three: get to the props table backstage unobserved. As before, the tables were laid out with the props in the same order. This time he spiked the whisky and soda not the martinis. He swirled the cold tea whisky substitute around in the glass. The white powder dispersed and vanished. Folding the now empty envelope he slipped it into his pocket.

Stage four: retire to his dressing room with his tampering unseen, and soothe his nerves with a coffee, and await the arrival of the cast.

Having been through this routine before seemed to have a calming influence on Nathan. This time the agitation and worry of the previous attempt were completely absent. His performance on stage was almost perfect, in fact he seemed to perform better than usual. He was devoid of any nervous tension whatsoever tonight. In Cambridge the play seemed to move with a leaden pace that made continental drift look fast and hurried. Now time flew.

His main consolation throughout this second attempt at his nefarious plot, was that the unfortunate Jenny seemed to have fully recovered with no long-term ill effects from her lavatorial torment. Hopefully Lancelot would be the same. He just wanted him out of action long enough to take over and prove his worth, thereby making him the better choice for leading man.

The scene before the planned poisoning did not require him or Deidre. They both retired to their respective dressing rooms to change into the tennis costumes required for their next entrance. They arrived almost simultaneously backstage, and stood side by side, just out of sight stage left. Nathan in white shorts and a Fred Perry shirt, Deidre in a short white cotton tennis dress. They both held weighty old fashioned, lacquered wooden rackets. To add to their weight, they were both encased in those heavy duty wooden protective presses so common in Nathan's past. Lancelot was a stickler for accuracy, and had decreed at the start of the tour that the light, modern carbon fibre rackets would look anachronistic for the setting of the play, hence the heavy vintage wooden ones from the prop table. Moriarty fidgeted from side to side behind the two waiting actors trying to see what was happening on the stage. Wherever wolfhounds are they must be involved, or at least think they are involved. If he could not see the stage, how would he know if his vital assistance was in any way required. They all have a built-in, unshakeable conviction that their input in any endeavour will always make anything and everything function better.

On stage Johnathon and Penny reclined in over-stuffed chintz chairs. They were both frowning at Lancelot in their roles as the disapproving Colonel and Aunt Amelia. Joseph stood erect and stately as the butler, tray in hand with make-believe whisky placed exactly centrally on it. Lancelot strode back and forth, his legs strutting with determined indignation, declaring his unalterable intention to marry Abigail Willoughby-Smyth come what may. The cue for their entrance drew closer. Nathan glanced down and spotted that one of Deidre's tennis pumps was untied, the long white strand of lace straggling across the scuffed floor. Giving his co-star a discreet nudge, he pointed this out to her. She tutted and bent down straight legged to retie the shoe with a good safe schoolgirl double bow. It was at this point Moriarty's patience finally ran out. If he couldn't see then he would have to take action to remedy this deplorable situation.

Here the reader needs to understand that wolfhounds have no concept of either personal space or inappropriate contact. Let me explain. Many people have experienced the famous 'wolfhound lean.' This is when they stand next to you and place their entire substantial bodyweight against your hip. They will often simultaneously stand on your foot and take your complaining, stumbling sideways stagger as a sign you have enjoyed the experience. If the mood takes them, they will climb into your lap, especially if you are smaller than they are. There are few experiences more life changing than being sat on by a dog that outweighs you by a couple of stone. To the onlooker, your muffled cries for help, concealed by the affectionate hound, also serves as a good ventriloquist turn. So it was, when Deidre bent over, Moriarty applied the time-honoured wolfhound solution to people who were in his way. He shoved.

To understand the spectacular events of the next few seconds, it helps if you grew up in the 1960's or 70's. Any child from that era will remember a board game called Mousetrap. Progress around the board allowed the players to construct an elaborate multi stage mousetrap. The setting off of this 'Heath Robinson' device being the climax of the game, as the various elements each in turn triggered the next part, until the mouse cage waggled down the ratcheted pole it sat atop, and humanely caught the titular mouse. The events on stage had a horrifyingly similar pattern.

The first part of this exercise in disaster that the audience saw was the hunched, doubled over, tennis dress clad figure of Deidre, shooting onto the stage at some speed, arms flailing and screaming loudly. Deidre, although tall, was slender, and was vastly outweighed by Moriarty who used his bulk, and all four firmly planted feet to get her out of his way. She had absolutely no chance of keeping her footing. The arm flailing was her vain attempt to avoid falling over and using her elegant face as a brake on the floor. The scream was partly surprise at being shunted forward, and partly shock, at the unexpected application of a cold wet wolfhound nose onto her warm bare leg; never a pleasant sensation. The weighty wooden tennis racket and press held only tenuously in her right hand, parted company with her fingers and scythed through the air across the stage. Its flight was terminated with an audibly solid impact on the left ear of Joseph as Shaw the butler. He was standing side on to Deidre as she hurtled onstage. Her scream had made him twitch in shock but he had no time in which to turn and see the disaster heading his way.

To understand what happened next it is helpful once again to reference the politically incorrect past. Anyone who was a child in the 60's and 70's would be familiar with the parent, teacher, or indeed any other authority figure implementing the time approved disciplinary method of 'a clip round the ear.' Those who experienced such a method of loving child care can testify that it is very painful. Therefore, when the spinning mass of the tennis racket hit Joseph squarely on the ear, the results were spectacular. Joseph hurled the tray away from himself and clutched his offended lobe. He then proceeded to release a stream of invective of such corrosive intensity that it caused every parent in the auditorium to place frantic hands over their children's ears. The tray in turn now flew twinkling and spinning like a steel frisbee towards the audience. The glass of faux whisky spun off, landing with unerring comic accuracy in the crotch of the Colonel, immediately giving the impression that the unfortunate actor had been struck with a sudden attack of stress incontinence.

The tray continuing its arcing flight, whisked forward and hit Lancelot just below the back of his skull, right at the very top of his spine. Sadly, at that moment he was striding briskly forward with some considerable vigour towards the footlights, and the audience. The spinning missile therefore caught him just as he took his final step. His momentum, and the fact he was only on one leg, and in mid-stride, proved indisputably the universal law that every action has an opposite and equal reaction. The momentum and whirling mass of the metal tray transferred itself to Lancelot, and increased his speed just enough to somersault him towards the edge of the stage. It was then that a second universal law, (possibly because it felt left out of the proceedings), took over. As he was no longer attached to the surface of the stage, and momentum will after all only take you so far, gravity stepped in and decided it was time to join the fun, and Lancelot plummeted head first into the orchestra pit.

The Kemp players had a compact and happy group of just six carefree musicians. Theirs was an undemanding job as they only had seven musical numbers to play and by this point in the tour, had done it so many times they could probably perform it in their sleep. This relaxed attitude to their job meant they were, with no music required for the current scene, all passing the time with games on their smart phones, or reading. They were therefore quite understandably a little slow to react when the crashing, stamping, screaming and swearing erupted from the stage above them. It was just as they were looking up that Lancelot hove into view, plunging down towards the unsuspecting drummer. It must be said that it is to the drummer's credit, that he threw himself and his copy of the Racing Times out of the impact zone with such commendable alacrity. His absenting himself from the landing zone did however give Lancelot a clear unobstructed path, and enabled him to land squarely on the drum kit. The sound this made, consisting as it did of splitting drum skins and crashing metal, was exceptional. He flattened the snare drum at the expense of breaking his collarbone. His head struck the bass drum a glancing blow of some power, and finished up wedged inside it. A flailing, trailing leg threw the high-hat cymbal skittering to one side. The top cymbal coming loose from the stand rolled across the hard floor of the orchestra pit with a metallic ringing tone. Eventually running out of momentum it gave up trying to escape the danger zone and rolled round and round in diminishing circles. Making a descending tintinnabulation note that sounded reminiscent of the climax of many a comedy routine. Wah, wah, wah, Wwaahh.

Silence now reigned in the entire theatre. There was only the now almost inaudible whispered swearing of the butler to break its spell. Deidre was on her hands and knees peering upward in horror at the destruction in front of her. Penny had covered her eyes and having regained her lost faith in a higher power was whispering a small prayer. Johnathon was brushing ineffectually at his soaked crotch. The drummer was staring at the ceiling, sprawled flat on his back, the sundered torn halves of the Racing Times clutched in terrified fingers. The rest of the orchestra had shown the exceptional survival instincts and self-preservation of all professional musicians, and were now cowering in the far corner of the pit. The audience were sitting in stunned open mouthed shock. Nathan and Moriarty exchanged a look of horror. Moriarty shuffled his feet and adopted a stance and expression that was the wolfhound equivalent of a shrug and a 'that wasn't my fault' look.

After a long minute the somewhat muffled, tremulous, but still commanding voice of Lancelot echoed up out of the depths of the pit.

'I am terribly sorry Ladies and Gentleman but there will be a short interruption to our performance tonight. Could I ask the stage manager to close the curtains please. We will be taking an interval now. On a personal note, if there is a doctor in the house could he make himself known to the company. Thank you so much for your patience. We will be back with you very shortly.'

8

STARDUST

As it happened there were two doctors at the performance that night, and both attended to Lancelot's initial care. They were unanimous in deciding an ambulance should be called, despite his protests that he was sure he would be fine. It was later confirmed by the doctor at the Peterborough City Hospital that he had broken his collar bone, his right arm and three ribs.

In the wake of his protesting departure Nathan as the new leading man rapidly took charge. In very short order he organised the understudies for each of the male roles as they all moved up one, with the obvious exception of Johnathon as the Colonel. The part of Shaw the butler now filled by Thomas the first assistant stage manager. Once order was established back of house he went out in front onto the stage and spoke to the audience.

'Ladies and gentleman on behalf of the Kemp players may I apologise for the interruption in our play. May I sincerely thank you for your patience with us. Although our leading man has had to go to hospital, in the finest tradition of the theatre the show must go on. The understudies are all in place and are ready to entertain you. We will commence the interrupted scene from the top so you will miss nothing of tonight's performance. Thank you once again, and it is my pleasure to introduce the second part of "Always Listen to Mother Girls."'

He exited to an uncertain smattering of applause and the curtains parted, the lights went up and the cast made their entrances.

In hindsight that performance was all a bit of a blur in Nathan's memory. It flew by. Afterwards what little he could remember was like a series of snapshot mental pictures. Random images stood out, like individual polaroid shots scattered across a floor. To the others in the cast, it was an incredible, exhilarating, unforgettable experience. Nathan seemed on fire. He strode across the stage dominating every scene. He seemed alive and vital in a way that they had never seen before. The audience couldn't take their eyes off him. He gave a performance of such power and veracity, and with such impeccable comic timing that the entire cast found themselves rising to the challenge he set them. All of them were carried along on his tide of brilliance. The audience were spellbound. This average comedy, with its hackneyed plot, stale situations, vintage jokes and cliched characters found sparkling new life being breathed into it. The entire company were all riding a joyous, laughing, crying, wave of emotion. Although they did not know it, what they were actually seeing, cast and audience alike, was Nathan's inner O'Toole bursting forth. O'Toole himself had once said "I'm not an actor, I'm a movie star." That night Nathan Stockwood was a movie star. Moriarty watched from the wings. If a dog could smile then he was grinning from ear to ear. While everyone else was stunned by this unexpected transformation in Nathan, Moriarty was not surprised at all. He recognised it for what it quite simply was. Natural progression, natural selection. Every pack has a leader, every dog has his day. Nathan had just become the company's alpha male.

In the following weeks as the tour continued along the length and breadth of the country, the play steadily grew into an enormous success. Nathan's stellar performance drove the cast to new acting heights. In town after town the local critics sung their praises. All this positive publicity drove up the ticket sales in a wave ahead of them, until every show was sold out. Theatre owners on the route ahead were rubbing their hands in gleeful anticipation of their arrival. For them the business in show business was booming.

As the tour drew ever closer to its final month in the West End, Lancelot although now recovered enough to take centre stage once again, stood back, and stayed in the wings. He returned, but only in his role as the play's author and director of the company. His business acumen had a long and serious chat with his ego, and the ego decided it would go on a holiday and leave everything to Mammon. So, he left the starring role in Nathan's hands. He didn't even attempt to change or give direction to what his new star was doing. When every performance is sold out an impresario's business sense knows it is on to a good thing.

Nathan sat once again in the Lord Nelson. Pint in hand, Moriarty perched next to him. This time the table had a buff folder laid in its exact centre. It was thick and slightly bowed with its bulky contents. Nathan had cut out every review they had received once he took over the starring part. Each cut out section was a torrent of praise for the play, and for his performance in particular. He had an appointment the following day with his agent. This folder was his ammunition, his leverage. Nothing would stand in his way now. He had for the first time in his career been the star, the driving force of a show. He was not the 'co-star', not listed in the 'also starring'. The Star.

Despite years of toddling along doing an acceptable job as a competent jobbing actor, he was gratified to find he did actually have what it takes to be number one. When he started as an actor, he was plainly aware that O'Toole was never second fiddle. O'Toole's ambition, drive and supreme self-confidence carried him through every obstacle and up to the heights of super stardom.

But along the way Nathan had lost sight of that ideal, that initial driving ambition. He had swapped his goals for the easy path. The comfortable path. The emotions running through him now had made a sea change in his personality. If he had to sum it up, he would borrow a line from Shakespeare, to quote Richard II "I have wasted time now time wastes me." Well time he thought wasn't going to waste him, not now, not anymore. He had found his lost ambition and was determined make up for those wasted years. He was going to get that part. He had discovered the importance of being Peter.

Once again, they drove to Norwich, found a tucked away parking spot, and ambled to Trelawney's office. They stopped to indulge the admirers of large wolfhounds, posed for a couple of selfies, and eventually arrived. On the way Nathan's thoughts were turning over the conversation he would have with his rotund Pickwickian agent, and the outcome he wanted.

Ms Roots was sifting through the morning's emails when the cacophonous thunder of Moriarty ascending the wooden stairs alerted her to their arrival. This time she felt she was more than prepared for them. They had booked their appointment with her boss directly by phone, and although last time that meant she had been unaware of their appointment, this time she had overheard her employer's side of the conversation. This time she was ready for Mr Nathan lounge lizard Stockwood. There would be no simpering, and definitely no giggling. She was a professional.

Moriarty entered first. Gripped in his jaw was a single red rose. Strutting forward with graceful confident dignity he dropped it on the desk in front of her, then sat down and gave her a wise knowing look. It had taken Nathan several hours of training, and a prodigious number of biscuits to get Moriarty to agree to do this trick. Moriarty on the other hand did not really consider it a trick for which he needed training. He had understood immediately what Nathan wanted him to do, but initially he had felt it beneath his dignity. However, he quickly realised 'training' was in fact an excellent way to get more biscuits, and so, with the native cunning of all wolfhounds he had taken full advantage of the situation. This led to the extended amount of time in which he consistently got it very slightly wrong and had to be encouraged to try it again, and do it better, all with the incentive of 'treats.'

On Nathan's previous visit he had been deeply engrossed in his plans, and had therefore understandably been a little distracted. Afterwards, running the events back in his mind he had the feeling that he may have upset Ms Roots. Like most men when trying to understand things from the female perspective, he was completely unaware of why, or how he had distressed her. His male intuition nonetheless had picked up that something was wrong. The rose trick he felt sure should amuse and hopefully mollify her.

Ms Roots was so taken aback by this routine that she failed at first to even spot Nathan standing next to Moriarty. When she eventually registered his presence, she had no time to react. Nathan smiled indulgently at her.

'Pussycat you are as always irresistible. Don't worry we know the way.'

With that he and Moriarty went straight into Trelawney's office. The reception was for a moment utterly still and quiet as the stunned professional sat clutching the single rose and smiling. A few seconds ticked by, then she swallowed. The humiliation continued she thought, simpering, then giggling, now smiling like a lovestruck teenager. Was there no end to the indignities that pompous man would subject her to?

In Trelawney's office things were not going the way Nathan had envisioned them. He was therefore definitely a rabbit of negative euphoria. Although being full of congratulations and praise at Nathan's success in the starring role, Trelawney had the unenviable task of explaining to his enthused actor that there was no new starring role ready and waiting for him. Nathan had felt sure that now the doors would be open to him.

'It's no good sulking dear boy,' reasoned his agent. 'Yes, you were a resounding success, but one swallow doesn't make a Summer. You need more than just one triumph. Plus, you are contractually obliged to be in the Norwich panto next. Rehearsals start Monday.'

Nathan sat frowning, his face resembling a petulant child whose thrifty parents had denied him a flake in his ice cream. His dreams were evaporating before him.

'Look, I can see you are disappointed, but you have a good part lined up for you in the panto. As Baron Hardup you have several very nice scenes.'

Nathan's frown deepened. Several 'nice scenes' just wouldn't cut it. Because this production was a panto there was no way he could ever be the star. Cinderella of course was the title role, and female. Prince Charming the next big role in the show, although a male character, was naturally following the panto tradition and was also played by a female. He mentally reviewed the cast, and the various scenes they had. Running the production like an internal stop motion film he searched for a way in. There must be something he could work with here.

'Buttons' he shouted, jumping to his feet.

'What?' replied a confused Trelawney, momentarily convinced his client had lost what little wits he had left.

'Buttons. He has triple the stage time that the Baron has, a lot of audience interaction, and some really funny set pieces with the Dames, plus two songs. I must be Buttons.'

'But that part is already cast.'

Nathan stood up and strode to the front of the desk. He loomed over his now nervous agent. Leaning forward he planted two clenched fists on the varnished surface.

'Not for long' Nathan growled, face set and determined.

9

HIGH SPIRITS

Nathan sat on the terrace of his apartment staring out at the dour overcast distant North Sea horizon. The water heaved like a discontented child under a wet grey blanket. Moriarty was sprawled on the lawn on his back, all four legs in the air, head thrown back, producing a snore like an electric saw cutting through sailcloth. Unlike the laid back, comatose hound, Nathan was tense. He sat upright and rigid in a cane chair tapping his fingers on his knee. He had the same conundrum rattling back and forth across his synapses. The puzzle of how to get himself swapped into the role of Buttons was like an itch he couldn't quite scratch.

The Norwich Christmas panto was a huge event in the Norfolk social calendar. It contained the usual eclectic mix of performers. A smorgasbord of actors and 'media personalities,' all of whom were chosen to appeal to the widest demographic of the paying audience. Added to that were a sprinkling of local amateur dramatic semi-professionals. Once again, the "business" in "show business" had reared its ugly capitalist head. He ran through the cast members over and over again, looking for something or someone to use; somewhere he could insert a sabotaging jemmy to lever his way into the role of Buttons.

Nathan had met his fellow cast members the day before when they assembled for the first read through of the script. For the umpteenth time he reviewed them in order of prominence, hoping for inspiration to strike.

Cinders was played by Mandy Cedarwood, a popular actor in a current soap success. She was a bright bubbly blonde with an outgoing cheerful personality, but a London accent that was so dense it almost needed subtitles. She was a competent performer. Her experience in playing exaggerated characters in soap operas, coupled with her natural dynamic energy made her ideal for the larger-than-life performance required for good panto.

Prince charming was played by, Alyssa, a singer with three or four top ten successes under her belt. While she was not by nature an actor, her musical experience meant she had all the necessary upfront, thigh slapping, projection and big stage presence to make her a good choice for the part. She projected the right amount of power in her portrayal of the prince to carry the role with elan and vigour. Off-stage she was reputed to be quiet, withdrawn, private even, and was therefore likely to be hardly seen, except for rehearsals.

The Ugly sisters, Euthanasia and Asphyxia, were played by two highly enthusiastic local Norwich stalwarts. A pair of semi-professionals with almost iconic panto credentials, they always worked together. They specialised in panto Dames: Monty Garden and Roger Heskisson. They had been in every Norwich panto for the last twelve years. The show was their personal professional high point of the year, and they threw themselves into their roles. Improvising and creating new 'business' to make their scenes as manic and memorable as possible.

Buttons was to be played by Sammy Summery. He was a regular presenter on a reality show called 'Haunted Homes.' It was one of those programme's beloved of modern TV companies as they are both ridiculously cheap to make, and very popular with concussed, undemanding audiences. The show's simple premise was to take the two regular presenters, and pair them up with a couple of publicity hungry Z list celebrities who were desperate for exposure. Then they let them loose in a supposedly haunted house while filming them with hidden night vision cameras. Sammy seemed a pleasant, personable enough young man, although in all honesty he really couldn't act, and seemed to spend most of his time texting, or posting on something Nathan seemed to vaguely recall was known as Tweeter. His lacklustre acting and total absence of any comic timing whatsoever was at least a salve to Nathan's conscience, as he felt getting him out of the running would do the audience a favour. The difficult question was, how?

None of the other actors in the production seemed to offer any way in which to remove Sammy. Before this panto their paths hadn't really crossed. They all seemed dead ends as regards his goal of sabotage. No, he just needed to focus directly on Sammy. There must be something he could use to get him out of the show.

It occurred to him he needed more background information on young Sammy Summery if he was to replace him. Nathan had already taken the time to learn both his part, and that of Buttons. He was ready to put his case to the Director Crispin Fosdyke for assuming the role, just as soon as he could devise and carry out a practicable plan.

A name popped out of the haphazard filing system of his memory. Edward Fonsonby, known in the business as Ed Phones. Nathan was pretty sure he had heard Ed was working on the technical crew of the Haunted Homes show. He was a sound engineer. Nathan had met him on a number of productions over the years. They had a shared interest in wolfhounds. Ed had a wheaten female wolfhound called Wilma. Yes, he would be perfect. He would have the inside track on Summery. He could be the answer to Nathan's problem.

The regulars of The Lord Nelson were treated to a new and unexpected experience the following day. Nathan had called Ed and invited him over to have lunch and a reminiscence on past shared adventures. With this in mind he had selected a corner table with two settles positioned at right angles rather than his usual spot. On one settle sat Nathan and Moriarty. At the other sat Ed and Wilma. One wolfhound was a familiar sight to the pub regulars, but not two of them sitting upright alongside their masters. More than one customer stepped into the dim interior of the inn and performed a double take at the sight of Ed and Nathan looking like they were taking lunch with two Wookies.

The four friends, human and canine spent a relaxing lunch catching up. Gossip was shared, ale was drunk and most importantly of all from the wolfhound perspective chips were consumed.

In time Nathan gently steered the conversation round to Sammy Summery.

'Funnily enough my next engagement is with someone you know. Sammy Summery. You work on that 'Haunted Homes' series with him, don't you?' He asked with a disingenuous expression of complete and utter innocence.

'Him?' replied Ed, a little surprised. 'Oh yes I know him alright.'

'He is in my latest production. Cinderella at the Theatre Royal in Norwich this year. He seems a nice enough chap, but a little out of his depth in a panto.'

'Well, yes, he's OK. Though to tell the truth I'm surprised he is in that sort of thing at all. I wouldn't have thought he could act for toffee. Probably the idea of his agent. Trying to raise his profile and get him more work. As I say, pleasant enough, but not the brightest of chaps. What my old Dad would call one can short of a six pack. They only have him on the haunted show because he is as nervous as a long-tailed cat in a room full of rocking chairs.'

This seemed promising thought Nathan. He decided to dig a little deeper. So, he frowned, and asked 'How is being nervous a good thing?'

Ed chuckled. 'You have to understand the genre. You see these shows only work if the 'on screen' talent are genuinely frightened. It really doesn't work if they fake it. The presenters aren't actors, and the guests are usually Z list celebrities and can't act well either. So, you need to plough the field beforehand so to speak.

Let me break it down for you. What you do is you get easily influenced and slightly suggestible persons, and put them in a pitch-black old house, and equip them with the lowest power torches money can buy. To make sure you get the kind of telly you are after you have to get them in the right state of mind. Basically, before you send them in you prime the pump. In advance of the shoot, they get a briefing pack, and a preproduction meeting full of information of a suitably gothic spine-chilling nature. It gives them the back history of ghostly goings on in the house selected for that episode. Once they are properly wound up and mentally waiting for something spooky, you send them in and film them with night vision cameras. We select the places we film in very carefully. Most of these are old buildings that are deserted, and have been for years. They are cold and they are damp. We come along some days before and rig them up with remote mikes, and cameras. When our stars go in the net result is the temperature inside the building goes up just enough to start things creaking. You know what old houses are like, full of odd sounds. Creaks, squeaks and groans galore. We've even had doors slowly shut on their own as the temperature changes. With highly suggestible people it guarantees good TV, especially with people like Sammy. He is a naturally nervous person who screams really easily and very loudly. By the end of a shoot, he's usually nearly prostrate. The production company have even laid on a counsellor to help him cope with the anxiety. He only keeps coming back because he couldn't make money like that anywhere else.'

Nathan and Ed laughed heartily at this explanation.

'Well, what happens if there are no 'ghostly' happenings? Surely that must waste a fair bit of money,' asked Nathan.

Ed laughed even louder.

'No, here's the really sneaky bit. No sane production company is going to throw money at a shoot that doesn't deliver ghostly goods. So along with the mikes and cameras we fit some small, discreet remote controlled Bluetooth speakers. These things are just basically small black cubes; they never spot them. If the filming looks like it's going to be a washout for ghostly happenings, the director just gets me to play a few carefully selected sound effect noises through the speakers. That will always ginger them up. Once you do that a few times their imagination takes over and they start jumping at anything, even stuff that isn't there. It really doesn't take a lot to push them over the edge, and let their minds run away with them. Just a few sounds played to these already nervous celebs and their own imagination does the rest. Then we just sit back and film the resultant panic. In reality after five series of this show we have never actually had a single genuine ghostly event. Every time it is nervous presenters and guests getting the wind up over nothing. However, their on-camera panicking leaves the audience with an ambiguous viewing experience. Did they see something? Was it just their imagination? A few hours of careful and creative work in the editing room and we have a dirt cheap, prime time bit of telly.'

Nathan leaned in and whispered conspiratorially,

'What sort of effects? Where do you get them from?'

'Oh, come on, you know me. I am the ultimate super techy nerdy geek. Which, when you think about it is probably why I'm still single. I've got a huge collection of sound effects at home. Probably, the biggest digital sound effect archive outside of a major studio. Of course, the majority of them fall into the 'Hammer Horror' category. Creaking hinges, rattling chains, clumping footsteps, manic laughter, scrabbling claws, low moans, evil chuckles, muffled distant screams, thunder, invisible horses galloping across the cobbles. That pretty much guarantees me a permanent place on the show. They know I've got any effect they need. Gets me a nice bonus added to my pay for every show. When it comes to sound effects, you name it I've got it.'

Nathan took a ruminative sip of ale.

'Any chance I could borrow some of this gear?' Nathan asked, putting on his most innocent expression.

10

SHERLOCK HOLMES AND THE VALLEY OF FEAR

Just two days later Ed rang the bell of Nathan's apartment. He had come to deliver a set of wireless speakers and a tablet to control them. While the delivery took only a few minutes, it did however take considerably longer for him to induct Nathan into the arcane arts of modern technology. Nathan had an inbuilt Luddite aversion to many of the trappings of modern life. Chief amongst them was his assiduously avoiding anything labelled 'digital.' His focus on his profession of actor meant he had an obsession with the correct use of language. In his opinion 'digital' was one of the most awful misnomers of the modern world. He firmly held the view that any of man's inventions from the stone club to the smartphone should be classified as digital, as it was impossible to operate them with anything other than one's digits.

After nearly three hours of patient, careful explanation, and then backtracking to explain it again in simpler terms, Nathan had finally grasped the basic concepts. A slightly careworn and tired Ed eventually left him poking at the screen of the tablet. Nathan looked rather like a stone age man confronted with that mad new invention called the wheel, and was definitely not liking the look of it. In fact, if asked, he was pretty sure that no good would come of it whatsoever.

Moriarty by contrast sat head cocked to one side contemplating all of this with happy interest. He had enjoyed watching them place the speakers round the room and then send strange noises to each one in turn. He had amused himself by going to each speaker when it made a noise and giving it his hard stare. Unlike Nathan he had worked out the principle quite quickly. Moriarty got vast entertainment from watching Nathan with furrowed brow muttering in techno phobic frustration, while a head clutching, gently admonishing Ed went back over the instructions for what seemed like the millionth time. Moriarty's quick, intelligent grasping of the technology, proved beyond reasonable doubt that if a wolfhound had an opposable thumb, we would all be calling them sir, and biscuits would be the currency of the realm.

The tablet was pre-loaded with a comprehensive sound library, each and every clip could be individually selected and sent at will to any one of the six speakers. Before Ed had left, he had got Nathan to select the sounds he felt he might need, and place them in a separate folder with each sound listed alphabetically. This he hoped would make it idiotproof, even for Nathan.

By the evening Nathan had begun to feel quietly confident. He had labelled each of the six speakers with a small painted number, applied with a fine artist's brush. He felt competent enough in his control of the tablet to now start to plan where he would potentially place each speaker backstage, and which possible sounds he would send to them. He intended to use the next few days to improve both his technical skills and lay the foundations of his scheme by planting just the right uncanny story in Sammy's mind. The technical side now firmly set and ready, he just needed to choose a suitable story. He needed something that would engage Sammy's imagination and push him over the edge.

The Theatre Royal Norwich is a beautiful old art deco building in the centre of the city. It proudly boasts its status as one of the oldest established theatres in the country. It has a modern stylish building adjacent to it called Norwich Theatre Stage Two. This is a dedicated workshop and rehearsal space in which productions such as the annual inhouse panto can be prepared. It was here the cast met for the first proper series of rehearsals. This space was a considerable step up from the drab village halls and forgettable community centres Nathan often had to frequent. Smart, modern, clean, fully equipped and best of all without the background accumulated grime and layers of unpleasant odours of those less suitable venues.

The only real drawback was that the urn was now a vending machine, and so was the source of food. Gone were the biscuits, cheap or expensive. Such delights were conspicuous by their absence. This was a major blow to Moriarty. He took his dietary requirements very seriously. There needed to be a suitable number of biscuits in his daily diet. He therefore took this retrograde step very much to heart. As a result, he sulked the entire morning. Instead of inflicting his company on the cast members, as he would usually do on the first day of any rehearsal, he retreated to a warm corner and lay down. With his head resting on his front paws, he ruminated on what was in his considered opinion, quite obviously the start of the collapse of modern civilisation.

The morning was spent in once again reading through the script from start to finish. At lunch the doors to the rehearsal room opened and a group of young staff members trooped in with tables. Once these had been set up, they were then filled with a cold lunch that was copiously arrayed on them. Salad, bread, a selection of meats plus the obligatory vegetarian and vegan options.

Moriarty's head came up. This he considered was more like it. While the lack of biscuits was still a serious issue, the provision of free savoury foods went some way to redressing the balance. He got to his feet as quickly as he could while still trying to project an air of dignified, nonchalant disinterest. The cast members filled plates with a selection of comestibles, and settled in to restore their tissues after the exertions of the morning. Moriarty went from one to another and introduced himself, then he turned on the charm. He delicately nibbled beef, pork, ham or chicken, and even cheese from one actor's fingers after another. This caused endless hilarity as each performer in turn was entranced by his refined demeanour and table manners.

He spent an inordinate amount of time with Monty and Roger as they had loaded their plates with that most perfect of all savoury pastries, sausage rolls. In fact, he patronised their company to such an extent that they had to return to the table and top up their plates, as they discovered he had an apparent limitless capacity for this particular snack. The only performers he ignored were those poor deluded souls who selected the non-meat alternatives. These were almost exclusively from the show's dancers. Their determination to remain sylphlike required iron dietary discipline. Where food was concerned your culinary choice dictated just how much your wolfhound loved you.

Nathan watched Moriarty at work with utter admiration. He had always possessed the ability to provoke very definite feelings in everyone he met. Most were entranced. Their faces lit up and they fawned over him. Nathan recalled one elderly, stout lady in Beccles market place who had got on her knees and kissed Moriarty's face repeatedly while cooing at him. Moriarty to his credit took this in the spirit in which it was meant and returned the favour with reciprocated kisses of his own. A few people, mainly the cat people of society, were wary, even sometimes frightened when they first met Moriarty. They would stiffen, and tend to stand on tiptoe arcing their torso away from him. His sheer size and shaggy appearance being more than a little overwhelming to those of a nervous disposition.

Nathan singled out Sammy Summery for particular inspection. He watched him with an intense if surreptitious stare. Nathan began to form the suspicion from his body language that he was not just a cat person, but definitely a non-dog person. From the moment he first saw Moriarty he had contrived to stay as far away from the great shaggy beast as possible. Constantly throwing him nervous glances out of the corner of his eye, he worked hard to keep his distance. Now, as Moriarty worked the room like a hungry politician seeking votes, moving from one knot of diners to another, Sammy carried out what appeared to be a convoluted, complicated dance around the room. He moved from one group of masticating actors to another. Sometimes he would move slowly, other times rapidly, particularly if Moriarty got too near. Each move in this intricate minuet ensured he was as close to the opposite side of the room from Moriarty as possible.

Recalling Ed's comments that Sammy was suggestible, easily frightened and screamed at pretty much anything, Nathan deduced from his behaviour that he had a fully paid-up hound phobia. At the back of his mind an idea started to take shape. He had been thinking for days about what kind of back story he could plant in Sammy's mind before bringing the technology into play, and scaring him out of the production. It needed to be something credible for Norwich and the theatre. Something with a local link that others in the cast might know of, and could back up with embellishments of their own. It wasn't quite there yet, he had a vague recollection of a story that might be perfect, but he couldn't quite get his mental fingers on it. The memory tickled at the edges of conscious retrieval but kept wriggling out of reach. He needed to do some research.

As rehearsals began to draw to a close for the day, Nathan collared Crispin Fosdyke, the director, and requested to go a few minutes early as he had an 'urgent errand' he must run. Exiting the Studio, Nathan and Moriarty crossed the road to the Norwich Library. The compact nature of Norwich meant the library was just a short walk away in the Forum centre. It always tickled him that the city of Norwich had a Forum because it was such a mix of medieval and Tudor architecture.

Despite its name one shouldn't imagine a classical space of colonnaded buildings. The open space was bordered by the gothic bulk of the Saint Peter Mancroft church on one side and the soaring modern glass and steel structure of the Forum building itself on the other. This housed both library and the BBC studios.

This time Moriarty had to wait outside as such places did not make exceptions to their no dogs rule, even for wolfhounds. Tethered to a convenient bollard where Nathan could still see him, Moriarty was quite happy to wait, as he knew it wouldn't take long before he would attract some admirers to massage his ego.

Nathan quickly crossed the open central exhibition area and entered the glass walled library. He paused for a moment and spotted a member of staff tapping away on a computer. He went to the reception desk. A thin, tweedy, bespectacled man looking not unlike a dusty bookish Nosferatu listened patiently as Nathan tried to explain the half-remembered story he wanted to research. The man smiled with the condescension of a literary guru and directed him to the section he wanted. A few minutes later he had checked out two volumes on the myths and legends of East Anglia. One was a bulky tome with a comprehensive run down of all Norfolk's supernatural stories. The other slimmer volume was completely devoted to just one specific legend, the focus of his new field of research: the infamous Black Shuck.

11

FAIRYTALE, A TRUE STORY

That evening Nathan pored over the two library volumes. He started with the single chapter that was devoted to Black Shuck in the large compendium of myths. This gave him a fairly good overview of the legend. He then moved onto the book devoted in its entirety to this specific myth. This he took his time over, getting the details and nuances firmly fixed in his mind. Finally laying aside the books, he took a notepad and carefully drew two columns on the bright clean paper. The first column would contain the positive points from the story he could use, the second was for the negative points that might hinder the effect on Sammy Summery.

In the positive list he swiftly noted several good points. Firstly, the Black Shuck story was a good solid narrative with excellent horror potential. Secondly, it was also a very well-known local tale, most people from this area knew the name Black Shuck, and something of the legend. They could probably be relied on to add to the drama of the account, especially if he made sure others were present when he recounted a suitable gooseflesh inducing rendition of the tale to Sammy. Next, he noted that there were a number of shops and establishments in Norwich that had Black Shuck in their name or signage. If his memory served him correctly the theatre bar actually stocked Black Shuck gin from the local distillery. These visual cues would help reinforce the story in Sammy's mind.

Laying the pad aside for a moment he looked at Moriarty. He was sprawled on his side snoring gently after his dinner of roast chicken. Nathan realised that Moriarty made a first-class double for the infamous devil dog. Sammy, it was already clear was not fond of dogs of any kind, and was indeed probably very frightened of them. He was also very suggestible and scared easily. He added Moriarty to his positive column. He picked up the pad again and gave thought to the negative column.

In the negative list there were really only two points. Firstly, Moriarty was a Brindle coloured hound not black, but Nathan thought with his great size, Brindle was a dark enough hue to pass muster. Secondly, Black Shuck had never actually appeared in Norwich itself, though rather frustratingly for Nathan's purposes he had seemed to have been seen almost everywhere else in the county. Nathan on reflection thought if he gave the telling of the story to Sammy enough drama and passion, plenty of performance topspin, then that point might be glossed over. Hopefully Sammy wouldn't spot the inconvenient fact that Norwich seemed a Black Shuck free zone. If it seemed Sammy picked up on this geographical omission in Black Shuck's manifestations, he could point out that Bungay church was only twenty minutes away, and the doors had burn marks on them from the visit of the flame wreathed murderous hellhound, marks that can still be seen to this day.

Satisfied he had enough good material to begin his work of gaslighting Sammy, Nathan prepared for bed. Lights were turned off and the front door was locked. Moriarty recognising the tell-tale signs of impending bedtime went out onto the lawn for a final toilet trip. Then after a last look around at his domain he ambled back in. Or, to be accurate, halfway back in. A wolfhound will never miss an opportunity to extract a little extra culinary payment when he knows he has you in his power. In this case he knows Nathan wants to go to bed. He further knows that before that can happen Nathan has to shut and lock the doors. This gives him an advantage. Therefore, planting his substantial frame half in and half out of the patio door, and waiting for the inevitable bribe is a good tactic. Nathan like all well trained custodians, carers, servants, and lackeys of wolfhounds had already obtained the spoon and the jar of chunky peanut butter. Moriarty hearing the unscrewing of the lid came in. Game, set and match.

Nathan's first chance to begin the priming of Sammy's imagination came at the mid-morning tea break the following day. He cornered Sammy in the corridor by the drinks machine. There were several other cast members jostling for position to get one of the hot drinks the machine dispensed. Like all such machines pretty much every one of the drinks looked and tasted the same. The only one you could possibly hope to identify in a blind tasting was the soup, and even that wasn't certain. The line between mulligatawny soup and coffee it seemed was a fine one. Still the cast reasoned that any old port in a storm will do.

'You are doing very well for a non-actor. Is this your first stab at drama?' said Nathan with bright bonhomie.

Sammy wriggled on the spot, trying to edge to a position where Moriarty was at least partially blocked by Nathan. He went rather pale and seemed to have developed a tremble. Got you, thought Nathan, you really are uncomfortable with dogs.

In addition to the tremble Sammy had it seemed now acquired a stammer. 'Y y yes, n n n not my field really. Bu bu bu but I'm trying my be be best.'

'Don't worry, you'll get there, we have quite a few more days of rehearsals before the big night.'

He paused here, and frowned solicitously,

'I say, is Moriarty bothering you? I hope he isn't frightening you? Don't worry he's a big softy really. Wouldn't hurt a fly. I mean it is not as though he is Black Shuck or anything.'

Moriarty with almost telepathic timing chose that moment to take a step nearer and give Sammy one of his hard stares. These had the ability to unsettle just about anyone. The recipient always felt he had been weighed in the scales and had been found substantially wanting. It wasn't that Moriarty didn't like Sammy. He was however well aware of the poor man's nervousness, and just wanted to ramp it up a notch, purely for the entertainment value. Wolfhounds do have a strong streak of gallows humour. After a few uncomfortable seconds, Moriarty turned away. Through the hub-bub of chattering actors, and the clatter and hiss of the vending machine, he had heard one of the cast members back in the rehearsal room open a biscuit wrapper. The hearing of a wolfhound is so acute that they never, ever miss that kind of sound. He trotted away in the direction of a more rewarding victim.

With Moriarty's departure Sammy visibly relaxed. His whole stance softened and he settled slightly as he came off his nervous stiff tiptoe posture.

'No, no he's fine, really no bother at all,' he replied with a total lack of sincerity.

He looked enquiringly at Nathan. 'What on earth is Black Shuck?'

With the bait swallowed Nathan grinned broadly at him, 'Surely you have heard that story? The giant black hell hound with red eyes, giant fangs and claws that strike fire from the ground as he stalks toward you.'

Sammy started to go pale again. 'You can't be serious? Is that true?'

'No, of course not'. Nathan replied with just a hint of scoffing. 'It's simply a story. Although actually it's a very old legend. Don't they say that all legends have at their heart some element of truth in them. If you think about it, every myth must have had a beginning, a kernel of reality at its core. Now let me think. See if I can remember it rightly. The first tales go right back to sometime in the eleven hundreds. Black Shuck has been seen all over East Anglia for centuries.'

Here Monty, clutching a steaming disposable cup with unidentifiable contents, interjected into their conversation.

'All the locals know about Black Shuck. My sister says she saw him once in the woods near Cromer. Mind you she's dotty. Takes after my father's side of the family. They're all mad as a bag full of badgers.'

'Wh wh what do the stories say a a a a about him?' The stammer had come back for an encore. Nathan smiled inwardly. The worm had definitely been swallowed, now to let the hook bite.

'Oh, you know, the usual sort of thing. After all that's what you do for a living on that show of yours isn't it? Visit all those haunted sites. Playing spot the spectre. Must be fascinating.' He paused just long enough to raise the dramatic tension.

'Well, let me check my memory. Yes, yes, I can give you one example. Back in 1577 I think it was, he burst through the doors of Bungay church during a religious service. It's said he was wreathed in unholy flames and he scorched the church doors. In fact, there are still visible burn marks on those doors today, marks that the locals say were made by him. Anyway, the story relates that he padded down the aisle, his feet making no noise at all.' Here Nathan slowed his delivery of the tale, raising the dramatic tension.

He dropped his voice into a deeper more sepulchral tone, trying to tap into his inner Vincent Price.

'Just the sound of his deep heavy panting and the growling and gnashing of his great fangs. His eyes like two great red burning orbs the size of saucers. Fur, pitch black and matted, reeking of sulphur and fresh blood. His claws scored the flagstones, striking sparks and fire from the stone slabbed floor, and yet, making no noise. As he passed, people fainted and screamed, fighting to get back from his evil presence. Everyone there knew it was a hound from hell. His great head darted left and right grabbing and dragging men, women even children from the pews. He ripped them to bloody pieces, scattering the torn fragments of flesh across the stone floor, spattering the terror-struck parishioners with blood and brains. Reaching the altar, he grabbed the two worshippers kneeling there in fervent prayer by their throats and killed them. He then turned and ran down the aisle and out of the church. It's said he disappeared in a clap of thunder. The same day, at almost exactly the same time, he appeared in the church at Blythburgh, even though it is about forty miles away. Again, he killed villagers and desecrated that holy site and when he left, it was once again with a great loud clap of thunder. This time it's said lightning struck the steeple causing it to collapse.' Nathan stopped, hoping he had got his delivery right. Although he had aimed for Vincent Price, he felt he had accidentally veered a little into Private Fraser territory a couple of times.

Thankfully Sammy hadn't noticed. He stood spellbound, mouth hanging slightly open. Nathan continued.

'He has been seen all over Norfolk and Suffolk again and again for hundreds of years. It is said he can appear and disappear in a flash. You never see him coming or going. Even if you do see him and escape unscathed, it is said that such a sighting is an omen that you, or someone you love will very soon die a horrible death.'

Sammy's face was now the same colour as his white cotton shirt and he had begun to sway visibly.

Nathan looked directly into the eyes of a man who had just lived every word of the story. His over excited imagination had played the tale in his mind's eye like his own personal 'Hammer Horror' film.

'Just a story of course, but, well "there are more things in heaven and earth Horatio" and all that.'

With impeccable timing Moriarty chose that precise moment to perform the famous Wolfhound materialisation trick, and appeared right next to Sammy. The poor victim did not know he was there till he felt a terrible intense crushing pain in his right foot and saw to his horror that Moriarty was standing on it. The great shaggy head looked up at him, eyes that others felt were warm and friendly, seemed, to Sammy to burn with an unholy fire. In retrospect, Nathan felt that it was a probably a good thing Sammy's foot was pinned to the floor by Moriarty's great paw. His substantial bulk stopped Sammy making a hole in the ceiling. The poor man's entire body attempted a vertical take-off with apparent planetary orbit as its goal. The scream he uttered passed into the hypersonic.

Nathan smiled. 'See, I told you, no one ever sees Black Shuck coming until it's too late.'

12

HOW TO STEAL A MILLION. (Reprise)

Nathan now began to put the practical aspects of his plan into action. Drip feeding horror stories day by day into Sammy's ear he intended to gaslight him. Step by step he would move Sammy out of the production, and himself in. By using one creepy tale at a time, he would reduce Sammy to a state of nervous collapse.

First, he spent a difficult hour navigating Ed's tablet. Nathan had confessed to Ed that he wanted to frighten Sammy into quitting the show, and so Ed had put a selection of 'Hammer Horror' type sound effects in a separate sound file list. This he placed on the front screen of the device. That way Nathan could find suitable sounds for his appalling scheme. He should be able to achieve this simply and quickly, at least that was the theory. Erring on the side of sensible caution, Ed had invested some considerable extra tuition on making sure that Nathan knew how to add additional sound clips to this favourites folder. He knew Nathan well enough to know that failing to attend to this detail would only result in receiving a lengthy phone call; during which he would be asked to try and explain how to do this whilst unable to actually see what Nathan was doing on the screen.

Now Nathan had chosen the Black Shuck theme to frighten Sammy he realised he would need some very specific additional sound clips. Fortunately, Ed was an avid collector of sounds. He recorded and archived sounds with the fanatical zeal of a schoolboy auditory trainspotter. As a result, it took Nathan quite some time to sort through the thousands of sound files, and then edit into the playlist the ones most suitable for his scheme. Eventually, after sufficient muttering had been utilised, and a lot of frustrated stabbing at the tablet screen, the list was ready. Nathan had also got Ed to put the script onto the tablet. That way he could legitimately carry it with him from day one without anyone realising its true function.

This complex plan needed to be carried out in separate, distinct stages. Each phase needed to be carefully implemented. Gaslighting Sammy might not be enough to make him leave the panto. Nathan may need to undermine him to the point where Crispin would sack him to ensure the success of the panto.

Therefore, for the first step, he needed to plant the idea in the director's head that Sammy wasn't really working out as a performer. Each day brought them closer to opening night, and if the main male performer in the production was letting the panto down it would put increasing pressure on the director to either get him up to speed, or ditch him. The part of

Buttons was in many ways a lynchpin role in the panto. It was a high energy part that needed to be more attacked than played.

Fortunately for Nathan's plan, Sammy wasn't very good. The cast, and Crispin the director, were already clearly unhappy with him. His delivery was flat and almost monotone. Added to which he couldn't project his voice, a common fault in many TV performers. They were used to relying on microphones. That was even more the case with Sammy. Filming scary scenes in supposedly haunted houses, meant he was more used to whispering than projecting. Heaven help anyone in the back half of the theatre as they wouldn't hear a word. His comic timing was only funny by its complete absence. What is known as the "so bad it's good" effect. Monty and Roger, the Ugly Sisters had several good, funny knockabout scenes with him, but they were continually complaining to Crispin that Sammy just couldn't get the physical comedy right. The only thing he was getting the hang of were the two song and dance routines he had.

Nathan had decided that rather than run Sammy's performance down, he would step in and 'help' with the failing scenes. That way not only would Crispin constantly be reminded just how bad Sammy was, but would also see just how good Nathan could be in the role. After all, there were enough critics of Sammy already. Rather than be just another problem for Crispin, he would be a beacon of light, a solution to his dilemma.

This section of his plan would also serve as a 'Plan B.' If he couldn't scare Sammy out of the role, he would ease him out by making him look hopeless.

It helped having someone like Crispin as director.

Crispin Fosdyke was the type of director that could only be described as highly strung.

He dominated each rehearsal with cries of outrage, and on occasion hysterical screaming interspersed with some sobbing over exceptionally poor performances. It would be safe to say he had a very short artistic fuse. His speech was invariably delivered rapid fire, and usually at high pitch and volume. He left no one in any doubt when they had let him down.

This morning Nathan and Moriarty came into the main theatre rather than the rehearsal building next door. Going in via the lobby they walked from the back of the theatre auditorium down the sloping shadowed aisle towards the brightly lit stage. In the mornings Crispin had started to take some of the actors to rehearse their scenes on the stage itself. It helped them block out exactly where they should stand and move. Today was one of the set pieces with the Ugly Sisters.

Set in the castle kitchen, Euthanasia, played by Monty, and Asphyxia played by Roger, were supposed to be attempting to cook a pie when Sammy as Buttons enters, and gives them some cheeky comments. This results in insults being hurled back and forth, which then escalates into a comic food-based fight. The scene was just starting when the pair arrived. Crispin sat some five rows back from the stage in an end seat of the centre aisle row. Nathan slipped into the seat behind him while Moriarty laid his head in Crispin's lap. Moriarty was very fond of Crispin. He seemed to find his over the top behaviour endlessly fascinating. Crispin looked back over his shoulder.

'Lovely to see you both. Let's hope he gets it right this time,' he said nodding in the direction of the unfolding scene.

'Thought I'd pop in and see how it is going.'

'Badly,' sighed Crispin.

Sammy got through his dialogue with the sisters with no major problems. He had no trouble learning his lines, it was the delivery that was lacking. Quiet, and without the right emotive beats, it sounded flat and lifeless. Opening insults traded, they were supposed to leap into the first bit of robust visual slapstick. The enraged sisters were meant to chase Buttons round, over and under the large kitchen table located centre stage. That didn't really go too well. Mainly because Sammy ran the wrong way around the table. Head down and sprinting clockwise around the table, he slammed into Roger who was galloping at full speed, dress and petticoats flapping, anti-clockwise round the table. With a muffled thud Sammy's head crashed into the deep cleavage of the obligatory large fake bust that must be worn by all panto dames. Roger visibly staggered as the wind was knocked out of him but just managed to stay upright. Sammy by contrast being short and slight of build, rebounded off the two rubber cannonballs strapped to Roger's chest, and shot backward as though hit by a prop forward. Landing on his back he slid several feet along the floor and disappeared into the wings.

Crispin put his head in his hands.

'I can't take much more of this,' he groaned.

Nathan patted him consolingly on the shoulder. A winded Roger steadied himself against the table, audibly wheezing and trying not to be sick, then a dazed Sammy tottered back into view, trying to realign his neck so his head was facing the right way. Monty marched to the footlights.

'Did you see that?' he shouted.

'We've been through this over and over again in the studio. Can't that talentless little twit get it right at least once? Can we please get all the way through this scene just once. It's not that much to ask. He mucks it up every time.'

'Sorry Mr Fosdyke,' mumbled Sammy.

'Can we try it again, but a bit slower? I'm sure I will get it right next time.'

'Alright, let's do the table chase one more time. This time at walking pace. We can try it faster this afternoon,' sighed a demoralised Crispin.

He sat back down as the three went around the table walking steadily, then doing the leaps, lunges and ducking in exaggerated slow motion.

Crispin turned back to Nathan while absent-mindedly stroking Moriarty's great shaggy head. For a man who was such a stylish dresser he seemed unconcerned by the growing damp patch on the leg of his fawn slacks from Moriarty's slobbery chin.

'This is hopeless,' he whispered. 'If he doesn't improve, I will have a mutiny on my hands. He knows his lines well enough, but he just can't deliver them with any real emotion or timing. Goodness knows how anyone past row ten will hear him. As for the physical stuff, well, you just witnessed that little fiasco. It would get a laugh, but for all the wrong reasons. No wonder Roger and Monty are going spare. Those two understand that being funny is a serious business.'

'I will try and help him,' said Nathan reassuringly. 'You must remember he is not really an actor. More of a presenter. He just needs more time and a little guidance.'

'Time is one thing we are running out of,' complained the distraught director.

On stage, the three performers came to a creaking halt as the lethargic chase concluded. It should now be the second part of the routine. In this section, realising they can't catch the young, nimble Buttons, the Ugly Sisters were supposed to be at one end of the long table and Buttons at the other. They were meant to glare and shout abuse at Buttons then start to pick up dough from a large bowl on the table and hurl it at him. He in turn grabs a frying pan and deftly hits each lump of dough into the audience like a demented tennis player. The part of the dough is played by ping-pong balls. It is an odd phenomenon unique to panto, that while in other forms of theatre poor performers get things thrown at them by an unhappy audience, panto audiences love getting things thrown at them by the actors. Sadly, Sammy's lack of physicality once again came to the fore. Ten balls, ten misses. Monty and Roger threw their hands up in exasperation.

Nathan felt Sammy was probably one of those children who suffered terribly at school. When sides were being picked for any sport, they were never chosen. Only being on one team or the other by default. Eventually as the last child standing, they would be assigned a team. His arrival with the unfortunate group would invariably be heralded with a lamenting cry of 'Oh sir, do we have to have him?'

Nathan walked towards the stage.

'Everyone, calm down, let me give Sammy a hand,' he called.

Clambering up onto the stage he stood behind Sammy guiding his hands and adjusting his stance they tried several practice swings. The retrieved balls were hurled again. Ten balls, ten misses.

'Keep this up and we will need a couple of Wimbledon ball boys,' muttered Roger in a very obvious stage whisper.

Nathan decided to indulge in a little more constructive undermining.

'Let me show you,' he said encouragingly.

Time to show off he thought. Ignoring the frying pan he picked up a long plastic baguette from the table and struck an exaggerated baseball batter pose. Monty took the cue and wound an elaborate baseball pitcher style throw. Nathan swung and shot the ball out into the stalls. For the next few seconds, the three performers mimed an outrageous parody of baseball. Ten shots, ten hits. Moriarty watched the balls fly overhead but declined to retrieve them. He considered that 'Fetch' was a demeaning pastime only performed by lesser dogs.

Roger on the other hand was ecstatic.

'Brilliant,' he shouted.

'Crispin, we must keep that in. Get the band to play 'Take Me Out to The Ball Game' as well. It will be a hoot.'

Sammy stood at the side of the stage. Shoulders slumped, head hanging low, his face a picture of misery and embarrassment. If a Victorian artist had painted him at that very moment, he would have entitled his work, 'Despair.' Nathan felt a twinge of guilt, but his now rampant ambition firmly sat on it until it stopped wriggling.

Nathan put down the improvised bat.

'Look, Crispin why don't I take Sammy out for a bit of a breather, and try to go through the scene with him one on one?'

'Would you? You are a treasure,' sighed a relieved Crispin.

Putting his arm round Sammy's shoulders he steered him gently in the direction of the Theatre Royal bar. It was just about opening time.

'Time to get a little shot of something reviving inside you,' he said.

Moriarty abandoned Crispin and padded in their wake. With Nathan bars meant drinks, and most importantly, they meant the possibility of crisps for Moriarty.

Nathan couldn't resist an opportunity to unnerve Sammy a little more.

'Hope you don't mind, but it looks like Black Shuck is coming too.' He chuckled.

He was gratified to feel Sammy flinch.

13

JEFFERY BERNARD IS UNWELL

Sammy and Nathan sat at a small table in the empty bar. Not many people realise the Theatre Royal bar is open like any other bar, not just during performances. As such it is an excellent spot for the solitary drinker who wants peace and quiet, but also for those who just want to savour their misery without interruption. Sammy was definitely in the latter group. He was nursing a pineapple juice in which a forlorn ice cube floated in lonely splendour. Nathan had a large gin. Not his usual choice but he took advantage of the fact that it was the locally made Black Shuck gin. He made sure he pointed this out to Sammy, and was again gratified to see him twitch in nervous reaction. Moriarty was sitting happily chomping the crisps Nathan fed him one by one.

'Look' said Nathan. 'Don't take it to heart, this is all new to you. it's just flexing your performance muscles in new ways. You simply need to give it more time. Do your best, that's all anyone expects. It's the old adage, turn up on time, know your lines and don't bump into the furniture.'

Sammy turned his glass round on the table top, the ice clinked against the tumbler as he rotated it. He sighed deeply.

'The trouble is I don't really know what I'm doing here. I mean I'm not an actor, or a singer and dancer. I'm just making a mess of it all.'

Nathan's conscience made an unexpected counter-attack and pushed past his ambition.

'Look, I know you feel like a fish out of water, but don't give up. You are getting better. You know all your lines, and I'm told the musical numbers are coming along well. Yes, you are struggling with the physical comedy and with your projection, but we've all had to learn those skills at some time. I can help coach you through it. I can assure you, you will improve.'

Nathan's conscience felt a flush of success as it stood on the moral high ground, but his ambition wasn't out of the game yet. They had a 'Devil Tempting Christ in the Wilderness' type of conversation. It went like this:

Conscience: 'That's better, that's the real Nathan. Kind, caring and supportive. Not a back-stabbing ego maniac.'

Ambition: 'Not really. It's just given him the perfect opportunity to gaslight Sammy.'

Conscience: 'Gaslight, gaslight, what's that?'

Ambition: 'Call yourself the conscience of an actor. "Gaslight," the film where the villain convinces the victim they are suffering from delusions and are going insane. If Nathan is coaching him, it is the perfect setting to play mind games with him. Sammy will trust the very person who is plotting his downfall.'

Conscience: 'You evil swine, how could you do such a terrible thing?'

Ambition: '(Evil, manic laugh).'

Ambition one, Conscience nil.

Sammy miserably thanked Nathan and said his goodbyes, then headed back to Stage Two for a rehearsal of one of his musical numbers. Nathan finished his gin then carried on with his planning. He took a notepad from his jacket pocket. Opening it he studied the floorplan of the backstage area he had sketched out the day before. He marked Sammy's dressing room with an X. Then he traced the route Sammy would have to take to get to the stage. The object of the exercise was to choose the best spots to place the speakers. He only had six, so he needed to be precise. Plus, he needed to put them in locations where they would work effectively, but would also avoid being spotted by anyone.

After some contemplation, he decided he needed two In Sammy's dressing room. Two in the long corridor leading from there to the back stage area, and the final two on the stage itself. In his training session Ed had stressed the importance of at least two in each area. One speaker worked well but two at opposite ends of any room or corridor would give the added effect of movement. Hearing a noise to your left then seconds later hearing it on your right, intensified the illusion of an unseen presence moving around you.

He checked his watch. It was nearly lunch time. The cast would be taking the opportunity of eating from the buffet laid on by the production company in the Stage Two studio. Any theatre staff would have decamped to the nearest pub for a pie and a pint, so it should be a good time to select suitable hiding places for the speakers. He and Moriarty headed backstage.

Starting at Sammy's dressing room he was pleasantly surprised to find it unlocked. Thankfully it seemed Sammy was the trusting sort. Closing the door softly behind him he looked carefully around the room. It was the usual bland, sparsely decorated and furnished work space of an actor's dressing room. Shiny washable paint, and cheap battered furniture that had seen a lot of mileage. On the same wall as the door was a long mirror, well lit, and fronted by a makeup table with a solitary chair. On the left wall a rail for hanging clothes and costumes, on the right a washbasin and small round waste bin. The back wall was blank save for a narrow window set almost at ceiling height, this ran the full length of the wall.

The window seemed the obvious spot straight away. It was a high slender affair with a deep ledge that ran along the whole length of the dressing room back wall. The glazed frame was sealed and not intended to be opened. It was too high to reach without standing on something, plus it had an inbuilt useless design feature. Someone had clearly thought that if it was a window, it should have curtains. However, as the window was too high to reach the curtains were not only fixed in position and could not be closed, but did not have enough material to stretch across the window, even if anyone had tried to close them. Not so much a functional attempt to achieve extra privacy, as a pointless decorative afterthought.

Nathan took the wooden chair from the makeup table and used it to gain access to the window ledge. He placed one speaker at each end of the window. He tucked them behind the now no longer useless curtain. Climbing down he replaced the chair and fired up the tablet. Time for a quick test.

Each speaker had its own rechargeable battery. Once fully charged it was capable of sitting quietly on standby for up to seven days. All Nathan had to do was select the speaker from the menu, press activate, and then just send it the sound he wanted. On receiving the pulse of the tablet signal, the speaker would silently power up and play the transmitted sound. As long as he was within a dozen yards it would work fine. Any further away and the tablet's transmission would fall short.

So as to best judge the effect he sat at the table with his back to the window. Selecting speaker one and sound effect six he pressed activate. To his delight a deep, low, ominous, animal growl rumbled to his right. Grinning widely, he selected speaker two and played the same sound. He thought the result was really good. The right to left selection gave the impression of something moving behind him. The large mirror in front of him was an unexpected bonus. With that he could see the whole of the room. Sammy would be convinced an invisible beast was stalking across the room. Even though he was controlling it, the effect of the unseen, menacing, moving, growling animal had actually made the hairs on the back of his neck stand up.

Moriarty had watched all this with interest. When the growls issued from speaker one, he went over and stared up at the curtain intently. With speaker two then following suit, he trotted over to that one. He decided more than a stare would be required, so he returned the growl with his own bass rumble. One thing he was sure of, he wasn't taking any threatening behaviour from other dogs. Even if they were invisible.

Next was the corridor leading from the dressing rooms to the backstage area. This at first looked problematic. Taking his time, and looking carefully, he paced back and forth the length of the corridor. Eventually he spotted his two best options. At one end high up just below ceiling height was an old, now redundant electrical junction box. Going back to Sammy's room he once again purloined the chair. This allowed him to reach up and place the third speaker in the space on top of the box. The cavity was just big enough to accommodate the small electronic device. The other end of the corridor was not so easy. A few minutes thought left him with only one viable option.

Pulling forward a conveniently placed fire extinguisher he slid the fourth speaker in behind it. Carefully examining the end result, he was reasonably satisfied it would only be spotted if you were actively looking for it. It was to his advantage that the theatre like many buildings in this day and age had equipped the backstage area with modern, economic, environmentally friendly, low energy bulbs. In this case low energy also meant pretty low light. This time he selected a different sound effect. Standing in the mid-point of the corridor he played the sound of sharp claws clicking across a hard floor. Once again, he smiled. It was quite unsettling. The two sources for the sound played one after the other added the illusion of something large and invisible moving from one end to the other.

He hurried now to the wings of the stage. Time was running out. He didn't have long before people would start to return from lunch. This area presented his greatest challenge. The stage was wide and open, plus it would have a constant flow of cast members and stagehands. Here he thought the speakers must be very well hidden to avoid detection.

Forcing himself to slow down, he searched carefully to allow himself to choose the right spots. Rushing was not going to help him. He needed calm analysis. It was then he had his eureka moment. It occurred to him that he didn't actually need to hide these last two speakers at all. There was so much clutter in the back stage area that he could just simply leave them in plain sight. While the stage itself was a clear open space, the wings and backstage themselves contained a vast array of equipment. Not only was it a mass of props, furniture and scenery, but the very nature of the work space meant that there were cables, ropes, lighting boxes and so on. In essence it contained all the equipment required to create whatever illusion the performance needs. With that in his mind, Nathan simply placed one small dark unobtrusive speaker stage right, just inside the wings, and one stage left. The only thing he took care to do was to place them right up against the edge of the curtain so that no one would trip over them. Stepping back, he surveyed his placement. Perfect, unless you knew exactly what you were looking for no one would think them out of place. Question, where is the best place to hide a tree? Answer, in a forest.

He ran a quick final test. This time he selected a sound file he had found by chance when searching Ed's extensive library. It was a low female voice calling 'Sammy' in a creepy, long, drawn out tone. Standing centre stage, he played both speakers one after the other. Although his conscience still grumbled in the background, his ambition felt the warm glow of an iniquitous job well done. A few days of Sammy being digitally haunted should see him out of the production.

Buttons would be all stitched up.

14

THE LION IN WINTER

Throughout the next week of rehearsals Nathan took great pains to always refer to Moriarty as "Black Shuck." The others in the cast (with the obvious nervous, trembling exception of Sammy Summery) found this amusing, and it soon caught on. By day three, virtually everyone in the cast and the stage crew were doing it.

Moriarty took it in good humour and happily responded to his new name, especially if they then offered him a sausage roll or a biscuit. He didn't quite get why they had decided to change his name, but he reasoned, "a rose by any other name" etc. Plus, he was very well aware how stupid humans could be, and he had long since given up trying to fathom their incomprehensible behaviour. After all, at the end of the day, he knew who he was so he didn't get uptight if they apparently thought he was someone else. In his world he was Moriarty, with all the subtle and varied nuances that the name implied.

Adding to this theme, Nathan took to regaling the cast with fresh Black Shuck horror tales. Some true, some the products of his vivid imagination. This consistent refrain of references to the Devil Dog gradually and inexorably ramped up Sammy's base level of tension.

Starting the following Monday, Crispin stopped rehearsals in Stage Two completely, apart from an occasional isolated scene with specific players. These, if he felt something was exceptionally lacking, would be taken back to the Stage Two studio and run through their parts in detail. Now each morning the cast would go through a full-dress rehearsal of the panto actually on stage. Lights, costumes, music and special effects, the whole shebang. All with the goal of getting them ready for Saturday's opening night. As the first night loomed ahead it was now time for Nathan to bring in the added horror impact of the speakers and their eerie sounds.

He played the first effect just after Sammy went into his dressing room on the Monday morning. Nathan sat with his door fractionally ajar hoping to hear what transpired. Giving Sammy ten minutes to settle into his chair and start applying his make-up he sent effect six, the low growl to speaker one. He didn't hear the growl, but he did hear Sammy's squeak of shock. This was immediately followed by the sound of the door slamming open, the patter of feet and then Sammy knocking on Nathan's door. His head popped into view through the half open frame, one long streak of eyeliner slanting across his cheek and onto his ear, testimony to just how much the growl had made him jump.

'Er, sorry, I know you must be busy, but is Moriarty with you?' he quavered.

Nathan raised his eyebrows in puzzlement.

'Moriarty? No. he's off following Crispin around this morning. You know how he loves watching Crispers, especially when the old chap is getting worked up. And, boy is he worked up today. Talk about new production anxiety. I've never seen him this...'

Sammy cut across him with an agitated nervous voice.

'it's just, just, I thought I ...'

'Thought what?' asked Nathan, donning an expression of angelic innocence.

'Nothing, nothing at all, I'm just being silly. Sorry to disturb you.'

Sammy slunk back to his own room. Nathan gave it five minutes then played effect six again. First on speaker one, then a two second beat later on speaker two. This time there was a loud scream, some muffled shouting and Sammy shot out of his room. Then his galloping footsteps could be heard thundering away down the corridor. Nathan slipped out of his room on stockinged feet, and swiftly followed him. He left his room just in time to see Sammy sprint around the corner into the corridor leading to the backstage area.

Peeking round the corner he saw that Sammy had stopped halfway down the corridor. He was leaning against the wall and breathing heavily, one hand clutching his chest, presumably trying to make sure his heart stayed inside his ribcage. With each shuddering breath he was demonstrating the deeply religious side of his personality by repeatedly calling out to the supreme deity. Nathan scrolled down through the tablet sound list. Number four to speaker four he decided. Sammy visibly jumped up off the floor as the sound of sharp claws running on a hard floor came from the far end of the corridor. Like a greyhound spotting the electric rabbit he set off back the way he had come, arms and legs pumping he headed back towards the safety of the dressing room and the lurking Nathan.

Choosing just the right moment for the maximum shock effect possible Nathan sent the same sound to speaker three. Sammy applied the brakes instantly. He realised he was now running towards the unseen ghostly Devil Dog. With a high-pitched ululating wail, he spun around and sprinted away, his feet seeming to barely touch the ground. Nathan returned to his dressing room. That should do for now he thought. The game was most definitely afoot.

It was quite some time later that a gently whimpering Sammy was led back to his room by the dresser, a Miss Mary Mousebucket. She was a kindly middle-aged soul, and had found Sammy standing trembling and muttering incoherently centre stage. Taking pity on him she had offered to escort him back to his dressing room. Such was his state of nervous collapse, she had to stay with him until he was fully made up and costumed.

After the deep shock Nathan had administered, he expected Sammy to be next to useless in the dress rehearsal. However, it was with utter amazement he watched Sammy give the performance of his life. He was word perfect, his comic timing vastly improved. The slapstick sections, though more than a little lacklustre, were still way ahead of his previous attempts. Even his voice was louder, almost reaching the back stalls. The plan had backfired. The fear Sammy had felt at the ghostly visitations had been turned into the ultimate adrenaline rush. He had stormed through the first half of the panto with consummate ease.

Crispin pulled Nathan to one side as the cast dispersed for a thirty-minute break prior to starting the second half of the panto.

He gripped Nathan's arm tightly.

'I can't thank you enough. I don't know what you did, but that was amazing. I think you may have just saved the entire show. Sammy told me you had volunteered to coach him. How you got him from useless to passable is beyond belief. I was all set to drop him and get you to take the role. I even had a local semi-professional chum of Monty and Roger all set to take on your Baron Hardup role. It's looks as though I won't need to now.'

Nathan smiled while at the same time inwardly seething. Well, his ambition was seething, his conscience was doing a small victory dance and chanting 'loser, loser.'

'I didn't do much really,' he muttered through clenched teeth. 'But don't get carried away. We have had weeks of poor performances from him. It could all be a flash in the pan.'

Crispin's smile faltered.

'Good point. Let's see how he does in the second half before we pass judgement.'

Nathan stomped away, mind furiously racing. Now what could he do? It had all looked as though it was working perfectly. Finding out he had been just a whisker away from getting the role was galling. Now he needed to combine both frightening Sammy, with wrecking his current ongoing performance, and he needed to do it quickly.

The cast assembled for part two. The first few scenes were played out. Everything went smoothly. Sammy wasn't needed until the first big musical number of the second half. It was a scene where Cinderella is in tears as she has been told she can't go to the ball. To try and lift her spirits, Buttons leads the chorus members playing the household servants in an impromptu ball of their own. He takes the chorus in a spirited song and dance routine to the tune of "The Varsity Drag." It involves much stamping, high kicking and high energy.

Sammy had done quite well in rehearsal with learning and performing this demanding number. Nathan did however remember that he was still uncomfortable performing it on the stage. His problem was that the Theatre had what is called a Raked Stage. This means it inclined down towards the audience. The slope helped the viewers see the performance from a slightly elevated angle. It did however throw Sammy ever so slightly off balance. For him hours of practice on a level dance floor went completely out the window on the slope of the stage. The incline wasn't really that steep, but those unfamiliar with it got the feeling they were trying to act on the side of a hill.

Nathan decided that now it was all or nothing. He had originally planned to play the sounds when Sammy was alone. Now however he felt it was time to risk everything on one toss of the dice.

He waited until the dance routine was in full swing. Sammy was on the far right, high kicking like a latter-day Tiller Girl at the end of a line of six prancing housemaids. Nathan sent effect one to speaker six. 'SAAMMMYYY.' Then he sent it immediately to speaker five. 'SAAMMMYYY.' With the orchestra in full swing the chorus girls didn't quite register the unexpected sound. Two of them frowned slightly and lost a little of their rhythm, but they quickly discounted it and pressed on with the dance. Sammy however jumped as though he had just been electrocuted. It was the same effect as when you hear your name called out in a noisy room, it gets your attention despite other competing voices. He didn't just stumble he went completely out of control. The unexpected sound of his name echoing in haunted tones combined with the discombobulating effect of the inclined stage sent him staggering sideways into the girl on his left. From then on it was like watching dominoes. Each girl tumbled into the next, their weight and impetus adding that little bit extra momentum to the next dancer in the sequence. By the time the last girl was hit, who sadly was the shortest and most petite of them all, the momentum was such that she shot off as though fired from a cannon into the wings with a loud surprised squawk, followed by a cacophonous crash.

'No, no, no, no.' The irate scream of the choreographer cut across the music. Egbert Entwhistle, Choreographer to the stars (as he thought of himself), surged out of the wings. He was a tiny, slender, birdlike man who seemed never to stand still, he was always twitching and moving with barely suppressed nervous energy. If the cast thought Crispin was highly strung, Egbert was on an entirely different level of hysterical tension. He went everywhere with a black ebony cane topped with a round silver ball. This was now pounded on the floor with rage.

'What are you doing?' he roared. 'Look, watch me.'

Striking a pose, he faced the empty auditorium, then leapt into the dance. 'Step, turn kick. Step, turn kick, Step, turn kick. Entrechat. It couldn't be easier,' he growled.

Sammy stood red faced and shaking. Chorus girls picked each other up and rubbed the various bruised portions of their anatomies, all the while glaring at the hapless Sammy. The sixth dancer limped tattered, and slightly dusty back onto the stage.

Egbert glared at the array of dishevelled dancers.

'Once more. From the top. I will not have you lumbering cart horses, you elephants, ruining my creation, my masterpiece. This may just be a panto to you but to me it is art, sublime art.'

Sammy and the chorus assumed their starting positions. Nathan smiled. Enough for today he decided.

15

GOODBYE MR CHIPS

The following morning as the golden sun cast long shadows across the multi-coloured, peaked canvas awnings of the stalls in Norwich market, Nathan and Moriarty strolled across towards the Theatre. As they came out from the canopied stalls into the open space of the Forum, they met with Sammy. He faltered in midstride, hesitant to join up with them. His natural nervousness around Moriarty causing him to want to hang back. However, when Nathan called a cheery greeting, the inbuilt politeness that afflicts every Englishman caused a forced twitchy, tremulous smile to appear on his face. He fell into step alongside Nathan, taking great care to be sure Moriarty was the opposite side.

Nathan deliberately kept the conversation light and well away from Sammy's uneven performance of the previous day. He chattered blithely about this and that; the simple inconsequential wittering that marks the denizen of "this sceptered isle" as the true undisputed world champions of small talk. Sammy, nervous of being in such close proximity to a dog that all too closely resembled the creature he had been having nightmares about, merely added the odd, 'oh' or 'I see.'

By the time they arrived outside the Theatre Sammy was feeling more than a little socially awkward. He had contributed next to nothing to the conversation, although Nathan had carried on talking without apparently noticing. Sammy felt impelled by his natural good manners to add something to the flow of chit chat. Just by the front entrance was a green plaque. On it the words "Richard Hearne OBE. 1908 – 1979. Actor, dancer, acrobat and children's clown. Mr Pastry made his debut at Norwich Theatre Royal aged six weeks."

'I've passed this sign every day for weeks now. The trouble is I've no idea who it refers to. Who was Richard Hearne?' Sammy asked.

Nathan looked at him aghast. Time to educate this poor, benighted soul he thought.

'Mr Pastry, or Richard Hearne, to give him his real name, was arguably one of the greatest performers of all time. I grew up watching him. He made so many TV and film appearances I couldn't count them. He was a natural comic. An incredibly gifted acrobat who performed all his own stunts, even in his later years. When I was a child, every Saturday morning my mother gave me some money and sent me off to the ABC Cinema, mainly I suspect to get me out from under her feet. Off I would go, along with just about every other child in the town.

We were all part of the ABC Minors club. We watched cartoons, The Three Stooges, Flash Gordon, Buck Rogers, Tarzan, Old Mother Riley and, best of all in my opinion, Mr Pastry. When I watched him, I would laugh so hard I wept, I clutched my ribs and quite literally slid out of my seat onto the sticky floor. Mr Pastry made me helpless with laughter.'

He paused, slightly misty eyed with recollections of simpler times.

'However good any of us in this production might be, we are nowhere near his level of magical comic performance.'

The trio worked their way round to the back of the theatre. Nodding to the doorman who seemed to be puzzling over a book entitled "Gordian Knots for Beginners." They entered the maze of dimly lit corridors. Sammy became increasingly nervous as they drew closer to the dressing rooms. When they entered the corridor where Nathan had speakers three and four concealed, he slowed his pace a little so that he dropped slightly behind Sammy and activated the tablet. Quickly selecting sound seven he sent it to speaker three just ahead of them. A low evil chuckle echoed from the hard walls and floor. Sammy froze mid-stride, one foot wobbling just above the ground.

'Did you hear that?' squeaked Sammy.

Nathan looked around dramatically. 'Hear what?'

'Nothing,' a chastened Sammy whispered. 'Nothing, I guess it's just my imagination, again.'

Throughout the remainder of that week Nathan drip fed selected spooky sounds to Sammy. Just two or three each day. His goal was to slowly and steadily ramp up the level of nervous tension. Sometimes his dressing room, sometimes the corridor, even on the stage. The poor man became increasingly unsettled. Nervous and twitchy he began to jump at almost any and every little thing. Once he had pushed Sammy to the edge of nervous collapse, he would pull out all the stops just after the opening night. If all went according to plan, he could bring everything to a climax and, hopefully, push Sammy over the edge.

Deep inside his mind his conscience grumbled and complained, periodically breaking out into lengthy lectures on the villainy of his actions. His ambition however fought a constant rear-guard action, taking great pains to present plausible justification for his behaviour. Nathan didn't want to bring any real lasting harm to Sammy, he just wanted to get him to give up the role of Buttons so he could step in and save the panto. According to his ambition it was actually a good thing he was doing.

An unexpected bonus to this war of attrition on Sammy's nerves came from Moriarty. Thinking about it after the climactic events, Nathan realised he should have seen it coming. Wolfhounds seem to have as part of their DNA the concept that any activity, no matter how important or trivial, will always go better with their supervision and assistance. Over the years Nathan had seen a number of workmen come and go from his apartment. Perhaps the central heating died, the Aga needed servicing, a carpet was being laid or decorating was required. In each and every case the visitor was greeted by Moriarty who weighed them up intently. Then while they worked, he would sit behind them watching. Then, at appropriate intervals he would stand up, insert his substantial frame between them and whatever they were working on. After several seconds of intense scrutiny of their labours, he would step back and give a small nod, thereby setting his authoritative seal of approval on the quality of the work.

A variation on this theme was now played out with Sammy. Moriarty became very acutely aware of Sammy's nervous state. Frankly, he could literally smell Sammy's fear pouring out of him. He therefore decided to make himself available to Sammy as a steadying influence. An oversized Therapy Dog as it were. In the parlance of our American friends, he was "there for him." Moriarty found it strange that Sammy didn't seem to really appreciate the benefit of this self-sacrificing support. In fact, he seemed to become even more nervous. Every time the solicitous wolfhound would appear, the timorous Sammy would make haste to be elsewhere.

To get Sammy to the right mental level of terrified exhaustion, Nathan needed to both keep him nervous and tense during the final rehearsal week, and make preparations for a suitably "Grand Guignol" event just after the first show. To bring this to fruition he needed a little more preparation.

First it was imperative to get a working knowledge of the electrical system. The carefully placed speakers and the sound effects were all good to go, and were doing their job well. The lighting would be his finishing touch. Bringing it all together, the mental priming, the unearthly sounds and finally the failure of the theatre lights would, he hoped, provide the vital tipping point.

It only took a little time observing the back stage crew to spot that one of the assistant stage managers was his best source for the required information. In every work environment there are a range of personality types working there. There were the ones just earning a wage. Then there were the workers. There would be a light dusting of shirkers, and most importantly for Nathan, the nerd. The nerd is the workplace equivalent of the train spotter or the Star Trek fanatic. They know everything about their job. Not just because they are good at it, or because they are particularly diligent in their duties. No, for them their work is their passion. For them it was more than a mere job; it is an all-consuming pleasure that they got paid for. These rare individuals not only have an encyclopaedic knowledge of their job, they love talking about it. A wise person once said "people love talking about themselves." The workplace nerd loves talking about himself and his work, his passion, his obsession.

Nathan's target very quickly stood out from the herd. He was the one who was the first to get to work and the last to leave. Even during his breaks, he could be found tinkering with the various pieces of equipment required to produce stage magic while still drinking his tea. To avoid any suspicious questions, Nathan made sure he asked about all kinds of different stage mechanisms not just the electrics. This meant a considerable amount of time had to be spent patiently listening to lengthy lectures on scenery, pulleys, traps, footlights, flashbangs, curtain equipment and a seemingly endless list of machinery, and all the little tricks in handling them. His eyes may have glazed over from time to time, and his brain cells slowly melted under the sheer weight of information he was forced to listen to. However, from all that talking he managed to extract just what he needed. Eventually.

As with the previous stages, the final plan was divided up into steps. Each step must be completed to successfully lead into the next.

Step one: At the end of the opening night, he would return quickly to his dressing room. He needed to be well ahead of his fellow performers. On his way he would pause to remove the solitary low energy bulb from the connecting corridor, where he had already placed the two speakers. One of the benefits of being tall with longer arms than average meant he could reach it without assistance. There would still be light from the next light bulb just around the corner. That light filtering around the bend would leave the vital section of the corridor in a dark, but navigable state. Being right at the end of the performance it was unlikely anyone would replace the bulb. After a long shift working backstage, even if someone reported it, the crew would hopefully leave it for the morning.

Step two: Once Sammy was back at his make-up table, he needed to pay him a visit. He would pop into Sammy's dressing room with a bottle of champagne, ostensibly to celebrate his successful first night. Nathan needed to be sure to engage him in conversation long enough for the rest of the cast to leave for the first night after show party.

Step three: As soon as he left Sammy, he needed to dash to the main circuit board. He would trip out the fuses for the lights on the stage and the dressing rooms. He then needed to speed back to be in range of the Bluetooth speakers to initiate the sound effects that would start Sammy on the road to his breakdown. If he was quick, he would be back before Sammy had removed his makeup and costume and had set out for the party.

Step four: The succession of perfectly timed sound effects, and dramatic lighting failures would hopefully send Sammy fleeing alone, and petrified in frantic panic. He would flee alone and terrified to the stage. There, in the half-light, the final sound effects would hopefully push him over the edge into complete nervous collapse.

16

CHRISTMAS COTTAGE

First Night.

The director stood quietly on the stage before the concertinaed curtains, watching the last of the chattering, laughing audience file out and away. The night had been far from an unqualified success, but was nonetheless passable.

Crispin consoled himself with the thought that they would get better as time went on.

As he expected, the weak link was Sammy. His performance was like the curate's egg: "good in parts." Crispin made a mental note to ask Nathan if he could help Sammy improve a little more.

Despite an average performance the cast got three curtain calls from a suitably festive and forgiving audience. As soon as the curtain closed for the last time Nathan set off for the dressing rooms at high speed. He was banking on the usual hand shaking, mutual congratulating, back slapping and hugging of actors relieved to have successfully got through an opening performance without any terrible disaster. This he hoped would delay his fellow performers. Reaching the corridor, he stretched up to remove the bulb. Writhing in pain he quickly removed his blistered fingers. He had just discovered low energy does not mean the bulb isn't still very hot. With a little contortion he was able to pull his jacket sleeve over his smarting fingers and try again. His tall frame and long limbs allowed him to reach the bulb, but only just. The bulb refused to budge. His problem was he was pushing it and trying to turn it on the assumption it was an old-fashioned bayonet coupling. Only after several seconds did he think to stop pushing and just turn it. To his relief it started to unscrew. He made several additional vitriolic comments on the subject of whichever nincompoops thought it a good idea to bring in an entirely new method of securing bulbs when the old way worked perfectly fine. With a final turn he eventually got it free. He managed to keep hold of it without adding too much extra pain to his burned hand. He scampered down the hallway and round the corner just as the first of the other actors came chattering into sight.

Dumping the bulb in the waste bin, he opened the cool box he had brought containing the champagne and a pair of glasses. Moriarty, who had been taking a restorative nap, made a small noise of request, and raising one front leg assumed the tummy rub pose. Though the clock was ticking Nathan obliged him with a vigorous rub along his ribs and stomach. Moriarty stretched his spine and arched his neck in pleasure. Even when it is inconvenient it is best to deliver the tummy rub. Failure will inevitably lead to a lengthy sulk. It is never pleasant to be cold shouldered by your wolfhound.

Nathan listened carefully, hearing the complaints of his fellows about the failed light bulb he knew exactly where they were. He waited for Sammy to arrive next door.

Hearing the dressing room door open he scooped up the glasses and bottle and headed to the adjoining dressing room. The iced dew of the champagne bottle soothed his bulb seared finger tips. Nudging the partly shut door fully open he strode in calling out joyfully.

'Well done, well done, well done. You did it. Your first live performance. Now you have got the first one under your belt it is all onward and upward.'

The cork shot out from his pushing fingers and ricocheted off the sink. Sammy beamed in satisfaction as Nathan passed him a sparkling glass. Nathan perched on the edge of the table and Sammy sprawled back in his chair. The next few minutes passed in convivial mutual praise, and frequent topping up of glasses. All the while Nathan kept an ear cocked. Listening carefully, he mentally counted off one actor after another as they made their noisy happy way out of their dressing rooms, and off to the after-show party. He was banking on the theatrical professional's irresistible attraction for free food and drink to empty the dressing rooms fairly quickly. Once he was sure they were alone, he gave it a couple of minutes more before pointedly checking his watch.

'Look at the time. We must change or they will start the party without us,' he declared.

Placing the empty glass on the table he briskly departed. Turning away from his dressing room he went as quickly and quietly as he could towards the back stage fuse box. To his relief, everyone was gone. Even the backstage crew had clocked off. Only the doorman would be there. Sitting quietly in his little office, he wouldn't stir for another hour when he made his final rounds and locked the building up. Turning on the small torch he had brought with him, he turned off the backstage and main stage lights, then finally the dressing room lights. Using the dim beam of the torch he headed back quickly, and stooping picked up the tablet he had tucked away out of sight earlier.

Meanwhile, back in their rooms, Sammy and Moriarty were frozen in place. Sammy called out.

'Hello, is anyone there? Look I'm still in here. Put the lights back on will you. Nathan? Nathan? Have you gone?'

Grumbling, he fumbled about on the table top and eventually his questing fingers located his phone. The light from the display was momentarily dazzling causing him to blink and turn his head away from its glare. Activating its torch function, he directed the beam of light around the room. Locating the door, he stood up and strode towards it. Shining the light up and down the deserted hallway he started to call out again when the words dried in his throat. Behind him from the dark of his empty dressing room there was a low ominous growl, then the slow click of claws on a hard floor. In his panicked state it never crossed his mind that as his dressing room had a rather nice mauve carpet that should be an impossible sound. Right now, his mind could contain nothing but every lurid detail of the tales Nathan and the others had been telling him for weeks. That, and a healthy dose of bladder loosening terror.

If there was a world record for the shortest time to run down a theatre hallway in the dark with only the dim beam of a phone torch, Sammy broke it. He scrambled round the corner. As he hit the long corridor leading to the back stage Nathan sent the sound of the growl and the claws to speaker three. Sammy accelerated. As he passed the fourth speaker Nathan selected the sound of the claws running, plus the sound of heavy animal panting. Convinced the beast was hard on his heels Sammy shot onto the main stage, and finally losing his footing crashed to the floor. Sprawled in the dim light cast by the auditorium exit signs, he scrabbled with desperate fingers for his dropped phone. Its light, though meagre, was better than nothing.

The growl sounded again. Now it was ahead of him. It was on the far side of the stage. Every hair on his body stood up. Sammy tried to do the same, but his legs failed him and he slumped onto the floor again in fright. Once again, the claws slowly sounded, coming steadily and inexorably towards him. This effect Nathan achieved by the simple method of increasing the volume. In his frightened state, adrenaline flooding his system, Sammy's mind raced for any possible escape. It was then his searching mind noticed a small green light at floor level, just at the edge of the stage. Right now, with just the auditorium emergency exit lights on it was the only other source of illumination. It fixed his attention. What was it? The claws stopped, and the light went out. The growl sounded again, louder this time. The light came on again. Even in his scared, panicked state his mind latched onto that light. The heavy panting sounded next, and the light made a third appearance. His terrified, adrenalin flooded senses picked up the fact that the sounds and the tiny green light were somehow linked.

Finding the strength to get to his hands and knees he crawled quickly to the edge of the stage. His fumbling fingers found the small cube of the momentarily silent speaker. Its little green tell-tale activation light came on as Nathan selected the unearthly devil dog howl sound. Sammy went from cold terror to hot rage in a single heartbeat. He lurched to his feet and strode on stiff angry legs centre stage. Finally finding good voice projection he roared in great fury.

'Alright, come on out. The game is over. I know what you are doing, and it won't work. I've found your little toy. You can't fool me anymore. Show yourself.'

In the silent gloom of the wings Nathan stood in open mouthed shock. His elaborate scheme in tatters around him.

When the lights went out Moriarty was at first puzzled but not alarmed. He lay quietly for a minute digesting this new state of affairs. Hearing Sammy's frightened voice he rolled over and stood up. His superior canine vision allowed him to see when a human would be blind. Heading for the door he went to help his nervous friend. He arrived in the hall just in time to see Sammy sprinting down the corridor for safety. The animal growl had confused him so he looked into Sammy's room. Empty. A puzzled Moriarty trotted off in pursuit of answers. He didn't rush, wolfhounds are rarely flustered and approach even odd events with a measured calm grace.

Arriving in the wings he watched as poor Sammy fell. The noises continued, and confused him even more. He could hear some other animal but could see, and more importantly smell no intruder. He reached the conclusion it was those little noise boxes Nathan had. His deliberations were interrupted when Sammy stood up waving something and shouting angrily. Now what was going on? He mused. He decided he had better look into this more closely and padded forward towards Sammy.

Sammy, now incandescent with fury continued to bellow challenges to his invisible tormenter. Hearing the snick of claws and heavy pad of weighty paws he turned to the sound coming towards him.

'Oh no. No more of that. I've worked it all out. I have your stupid little speaker. You won't frighten me anymore. I know it's all fake. There's nothing there, nothing real, just noises in the dark. Well, it won't work on me now. I'm going to find you and give you a sound thrashing.'

It was with this bold assertion still resounding around the auditorium that he saw the large shaggy form padding towards him. In a heartbeat he flipped back from hot anger to cold terror. His hand was shaking so much that he could not focus the tiny beam from the phone. As it jittered around the stage for one heart stopping moment it illuminated the vast hairy form of the great hound and for an instant, it reflected back twin eyes, glowing with an horrific lambent fire.

A sound reminiscent of a steam whistle escaped Sammy's lips. Turning he sprinted and leapt out, up and off the stage to the hopefully safe black sanctuary of the stalls. Landing heavily astride a row of seats and possibly damaging any future hopes of parenthood, he dragged himself wincingly upright. On tottering, unsteady feet he limped, with watering eyes, to the nearest exit door. Its green sign offered a comforting neon hope of escape from this nightmare.

He slammed through the double doors of the emergency exit out into the cold night air of a side alley. Looking left he saw the glow of Theatre Street and heard the hubbub of voices and music. With shaking legs, he careered down the alley rebounding from the walls, heading for release from this all-consuming terror. As he staggered out onto the street his senses were dazzled by an overwhelming assault of light and sound. It was perhaps unfortunate that Sammy had blundered out of the dark of the alley, and the terror of the theatre, into Norwich's annual Winterfest Christmas Parade.

Moriarty, somewhat bemused by Sammy's scream and athletic departure, stood for a second, then set off in hot pursuit. Leaping off the stage he thundered up the aisle and out of the exit door. Coming out into the alley he saw Sammy standing silhouetted against the brightly lit street. Turning, he set off trotting towards him.

Nathan watched in shock as Sammy, and then Moriarty fled the theatre. Emerging from his hiding place in the wings, he rapidly followed them both out into the cold dark night.

Dazzled and confused by light and sound, Sammy was unable to make sense of the Dante like scene before him. People thronged the pavements in chattering, shouting crowds. Down the street a column of brightly coloured and illuminated floats slowly progressed. Music blared, loud and insistently jolly. Alongside the floats phalanxes of be-costumed charity workers rattled plastic buckets. It was an awful, hideous collection of upright walking animals, cartoon characters and a selection of inappropriately shaped people dressed as elves. Sammy felt as though he had entered some drug crazed nightmare. Turning away from this vision of seasonal hell, he looked back down the dark alley. The open fire doors let a sharply defined, but dim blade of light into the alley. In relief against this dramatic backdrop, the great hunched form of the vast hound walked toward him in utter silence. In his hysterical state the shape of the advancing Moriarty seemed the size of a cart horse.

With a wordless inarticulate cry, he pushed, shoved and clawed his way through the knot of parade onlookers. Staggering on shaking, uncertain legs he lurched out into the middle of the road. Stopping in the middle of the parade, he stood swaying in utter horror, at the great lumbering vehicle now coming towards him. This year the centre piece of the parade was an even larger than usual Santa's Float. Towed by a suitably seasonally bedecked tractor, this vast platform was topped off by a sleigh in which sat the morbidly obese figure of St Nicholas. In the traces of the cardboard sleigh, attached to reins, people dressed as reindeer, cavorted in a pantomime of trotting. Santa himself, with the assistance of a sound system, boomed a constant refrain of, 'Ho, Ho, Ho, Merry Christmas.'

Sammy flung up desperately futile arms in a vain attempt to stop the advancing juggernaut. The tractor driver, who up to this point had been having a great time, was so preoccupied that at first, he failed to notice the now frantically waving obstacle in his path. The parade was a rare pleasure for the farm worker. Usually when driving the streets of Norfolk in his tractor, others, particularly car drivers, waved with an entirely different kind of gesture. It was for this reason he neglected to spot the obstacle in his path until almost the last moment. As Sammy registered in his peripheral vision, he stiffened and stabbed his foot at the brake. Sadly, in the process of trying to move his foot from the throttle to the brake his large steel toe capped boot slipped and got wedged between the two controls. He frantically pulled at his leg, trying to release the recalcitrant boot.

'Get out of the way' he screamed.

'AARRGGGHHH' replied Sammy.

'Move you idiot' he shouted.

'AAAAARRRRRGGGGGHHHHH' was the erudite reply.

'For pity's sake someone get him off the road' was his final shout. The tractor was right on top of the trembling Sammy.

At that point, with impeccable comic timing, Sammy fainted. The driver gave a wail of horror as the vehicle lumbered over the prostrate figure and flung his hands over his eyes. People in the crowd screamed, elves ran back and forth in panic, a Teletubby fainted.

Fortunately, the tractor and indeed the float it towed, had substantial ground clearance. The vehicle passed harmlessly over the unconscious Sammy and never actually touched him. As the vehicle and trailer left him behind, he reappeared behind the float sprawled on the tarmac. A bevy of elves and cartoon characters surged over to him, and bent solicitously over his unconscious form. Awakening from his terror induced swoon, it was a shame that the first face Sammy saw looming over him, was covered in white makeup and had a large bright red dot on each cheek. This was topped off with a bright green hat complete with a bell on the end. That was probably why he fainted again.

Moriarty and Nathan stood together in the sanctuary of the shadowed alley watching this unexpected climax to the day. Master and human exchanged a look of utter incredulity. Whatever else could be said about all this one thing was sure.

Mr Pastry would have loved it.

17

MY TALKS WITH DEAN SPANLEY

Nathan woke after once again suffering an almost, but not quite entirely sleepless night. His ambition had gone off to celebrate. His conscience however had stayed with him and told him just what it thought of him. He had spent the night being reminded of, and berated over his most recent misdemeanours. Finally, just when he thought he would get no sleep at all he had dropped off, barely one hour before dawn.

His life up till now, while not utterly blameless, was also not one of irredeemable wickedness either. After the initial enthusiastic, ambitious rush of his youth, and the competitive process of outperforming anyone else in the audition, he had settled down into his mid-level rating of semi-fame. There was no longer any need to push others aside and himself ahead. He was offered a steady stream of undemanding roles in the performance equivalent of that saccharine 'easy listening' music you hear in lifts and shopping malls all around the world. Not the most inspiring, life changing roles ever written or performed, but good solid middle of the road entertainment. Best of all it paid well. So, he had settled into a calm, satisfying life. He had no need to compete for roles. He couldn't even remember the last time he had to go and audition for a part. With this relaxed mindset he was easy to work with. He treated his fellow actors with kindness and respect. Until now. Now he actively manipulated and cheated to eliminate them from his path.

He had acquired a well-deserved reputation among his peers of being pleasant, kind and accommodating. A bit of an eccentric with Moriarty in constant attendance, but actually a really genial man to work with. A professional who just got on with the job. How that had changed. Looking back over the last few months he had hospitalised two fellow actors, and driven a third so close to the edge of sanity that he would probably need intensive psychiatric therapy for quite some time. And for what he asked himself. Just so he could get one, coveted role.

It was at this point, as he climbed wearily out of the dishevelled bed that his ambition returned. The internal rationalisation process began afresh. A series of very good reasons were paraded and displayed, proving that what he had done was really not all that bad. Placing a stifling hand firmly over the mouth of a protesting conscience, ambition made a spirited statement for the defence.

After one espresso and a brisk seafront walk with Moriarty, he had come to the conclusion that irrespective of the moral rightness of any of his behaviour, the fact was, Sammy was out of the production. If he didn't take the role of Buttons, the entire production would collapse. That meant everyone would be out of work for the next two months. A financial hit for the show's backers. A substantial loss of earnings for the theatre, plus thousands of disappointed children. In reality cancelling the Norwich winter panto was not an option. He owed it to everyone to make sure the show must go on.

He got back just in time to answer his ringing phone. A distraught Crispin breathlessly pleaded down the line,

'Thank goodness, at last. I've been calling you for the last half hour. Get to the theatre as soon as you can. We've had a disaster. You are on as Buttons for the foreseeable. Sammy probably won't be back for the rest of the run. I've already confirmed Roger and Monty's buddy to take on your role as the Baron, but he is coming in fresh and needs to get the role straight in super quick time. If we spend today rehearsing it, hopefully he can just about get through the evening performance.'

Nathan took a deep breath,

'Yes of course Crispin. You can count on me. Don't waste time explaining why Sammy is out. What has happened is secondary. We will need all the time we have to get ready. It's our responsibility to save the show. I will leave straight away.' As he put down the phone, he thought that one exchange had just proved how good an actor he was.

When they arrived at the theatre it was to a scene from bedlam. Distraught and confused actors milled uncertainly on the stage. Crispin strode back and forth in front of the stalls screaming contradictory instructions. Never at his best in a crisis, Crispin had slipped over the edge into rampant hysteria.

At the rear of the stalls Nathan and Moriarty stood in the half-light and watched the disintegration of the panto. It was then that for a brief moment the theatre and its surroundings faded from his consciousness. He found himself looking inward. A door opened in the depths of his mind. Through it stepped O'Toole.

'"O for a muse of fire, that would ascend the brightest heaven of invention! A kingdom for a stage, Princes to act." Time to take charge laddie.'

Moriarty stiffened as he felt the change in Nathan. It wasn't anything overt or obvious. It was just a subtle shift in his stance and posture. He was radiating a dramatically increased level of confidence. Moriarty looked up at his friend and frowned. What was going on? This was the second time this change had happened.

Nathan snapped back to reality, and squaring his shoulders strode down the aisle towards the panto pandemonium. He placed a consoling hand on Crispin's shoulder. At the same moment on the other side, Moriarty leant a comforting shoulder against Crispin's hip. The screeching tirade slowly wound down and the overwrought director gave way to silent tears.

Nathan whispered gently into his ear.

'It's OK. I will take it from here. Just go and have a break. I will go through all the scenes involving Buttons with the cast, and walk our new Baron Hardup through his role. It will all be fine.'

Crispin nodded, and wiping away tears of grateful emotion walked away up the aisle, and out of the auditorium.

Nathan took a deep breath. In addition to studying Peter O'Toole as an actor through his performances, he had also studied him as a man, as a person. He knew that while O'Toole could be difficult, especially in taking direction on his performance, one thing he always did was lead the company. He often was the glue that bound the cast together. That brief out-of-body moment had shown Nathan the way. This was now his task. He needed to don the mantle of O'Toole.

'Right, all of you who are in any of the scenes with me as Buttons disappear until after lunch. Be back here by one. I know the part pretty well. We just need one or two quick run-throughs to nail it all down. Those of you in the Baron Hardup scenes please stay. His replacement doesn't have too many scenes, but we will need to give our new friend as much help as we can. He only has one day to learn his part.'

He clapped his hands together twice loudly.

'Jump to it. If you are not needed right now, I don't want to see you. Monty, Roger, where is our new cast member?'

As most of the cast drifted off the stage Monty stepped forward.

'He's just popped to the loo. He'll be back in a minute.'

As he spoke an extremely tall, cadaverous figure entered stage right. He was around the age of seventy, with a long, lugubrious face and a mane of perfectly coiffed silver hair.

'Welcome,' shouted Nathan. 'I'm terribly sorry but I have no idea what your name is, however we are very grateful to have you with us.'

The man smiled a smile of such size and width that it almost looked as if his face would split in half. With a rich, deep mellifluous voice he declared,

'I am Tristram Montague Othello Carruthers. And I am honoured to make your acquaintance. You can call me Tommo, everyone does.'

Nathan and Moriarty clambered up the side steps onto the stage. Tommo gave Moriarty a wide-eyed stare.

'Now that is what I call a man's dog.'

'This is Moriarty, you can call him Mori.'

Tommo extended a large, long fingered hand and wrapped Nathan's in an engulfing grip. He frowned at Nathan.

'I have a big concern about this role,' he confessed.

'I know, we only have today, but we will get you through this. Trust me.'

'No, no. My worry is Cinderella, she is a very petite, very blonde, lovely young lady. I on the other hand am a very large, very much older man who is more likely to be her grandfather. You don't think that it will look a little odd for me to be her father?'

Nathan burst out laughing.

'Definitely not. This …' he declared, throwing his arms out wide and turning in a circle. 'This is panto.'

Tomo looked puzzled. 'Excuse me but that I know, why however should it being panto make any difference?'

'Think about it my dear boy. Panto is the nearest thing to pure theatre in the world. What's the line from Henry the fifth, the Chorus? "Pardon gentles all the flat unraised sprits that have dared on this unworthy scaffold to bring forth so great an object." We are the masters of the imagination, the engineers of dreams. In this show the principal boy is a girl. The ugly sisters are men. A pumpkin becomes a coach, mice become horses and glass footwear is apparently normal. Plus, panto is not a self-contained bubble. We burst out. We don't just break the fourth wall we crush it. Panto is the only drama in the world in which we tell our story in full, in the round. We openly acknowledge that the audience is there. We talk to them, we involve them. In panto the audience is as much a part of the cast as any one of us actors, and a little unlikely casting isn't even worth mentioning. You will be great.'

If possible, Tommo's grin got even wider. He looked like a human version of the Cheshire Cat.

The day seemed to fly by in a whirl of noise, action, excitement and organised drama. Nathan was so enthusiastic and positive that the entire cast rose to the challenge. Tommo threw himself into his role, and proved to be a capable actor. Best of all he was a fast learner.

For hours the auditorium echoed to the songs, shouts and dialogue of frenetic actors. With two hours before curtain up, Nathan dismissed them all with such heartfelt praise and thanks that every performer left tired, but elated, and completely confident that they could carry this off. Crispin was in such a state of nerves that they only saw him twice in the entire day. Each time he tottered in, looked around and muttered tearfully,

'Well done. I am so proud of you.' Then ambled away again.

The second night was nothing like the first. Before, the crowd enjoyed and applauded an adequate show. This time it was lightning in a bottle. Nathan's dynamic performance transformed the show. His scenes were such standouts that by the second half every time he came on stage the audience cheered, clapped and stamped their feet in anticipation. He simply outshone everyone else on the stage. Even though the principals were being upstaged, they didn't mind one little bit. Being part of such a show carried them all along on a joyous wave of excitement. It became a panto masterclass.

At the end, the audience surged to their feet and clapped for one curtain call after another. A grinning stage hand dug an enthusiastic elbow into Nathan as the cast went back to meet the thunderous applause once again.

'Keep this up mate and we'll wear the curtain out,' he shouted.

Nathan continued as Buttons for the entire run of the show. Sammy recovered, but never returned to the theatre. He went back to television and resumed his job screaming in Haunted Homes. He was however much harder to frighten than before. He had learned an important life lesson. It's a man's life in the theatre.

Two weeks after the last performance of Cinderella, Nathan and Moriarty sat once again in their favourite spot in their favourite pub, and sipped and basked in the warm glow of mutual companionship. On the table, as before, Nathan had laid the folder of his reviews. This time it was noticeably thicker. He now had two successful productions under his belt. In both shows he had been the reason they had succeeded: he was both a star, and an outstanding performer. Now his standing as a bankable actor was at a peak. His confidence in his quest was at an all-time high. It was now time for phase three.

Light comedy star, tick.

Slapstick comedy, singer and dancer, tick.

Now it was time to show he could be both dramatic and sinister. He was ready to unleash his inner villain both on and off the screen. For his next project was television. A high cost, high value, hugely successful murder series. The only problem was that once again someone stood in his way. Another more famous actor had the part he wanted. They would have to be removed. Two resounding, magnificent successes had quashed any guilt over his methods. Ambition was now firmly in the driving seat. Conscience, like Rapunzel, was languishing, locked in a remote tower of Nathan's mind. The feelings of guilt that had tormented him before were now nothing. They were dwarfed by the sheer size of his success.

For the first time in his life, he was not just an actor, he was a rising star. Yes, he had done some questionable things to get there. But there was much further to travel on this road. He needed this next upgrade in his career. He needed it to be on the bigger stage of national television. Yet another performer needed replacing. This time the gloves were really coming off.

18

COUNTRY DANCE

The morning post brought a thick envelope bulging with the contents of the script for his television drama role. Last year he had signed a contract to play a one-off co-starring role in a long running murder mystery series called Midwinter Homicides. This particular episode was entitled, "Evil Under the Moon." The series was a permanent fixture in the comfortable, undemanding light entertainment television calendar. It had been running for so long that the leading character, Inspector Barrowboy, had been played in succession by three different actors. Each new one replacing the previous performer in a handover episode of such preposterous, unlikely happenstance that it should have stretched the credulity of any viewer. It was a testimony to the numb, sleepy state the programmes induced in their audiences, that no one ever questioned these unlikely turns in the narrative.

By a curious twist of serendipity, the new star of the show was always a relative of the outgoing character, and was blessed with the same surname. He also, by a further twist of fate happened to be a policeman of the same rank, and it is of course a pure coincidence that he gets the job of his retiring namesake. It was a sort of Murder Mystery version of the Doctor Who regeneration motif.

Each of the episodes was set in one of the apparently limitless fictional villages in the equally fictional district of Midwinter. The real locations were chosen from the most picturesque, quaint, thatched, oak beamed, chocolate box lid, bucolic hamlets available. Each and every one of them containing the compulsory village green, oak beamed pub, duck pond and painted village sign post. The studio had a small army of location scouts continually roaming the British countryside in search of such places. The settings were a vital ingredient in these unlikely dramas, as a major part of the income for these programmes were from the overseas market. They were sold to a customer base of ex-pats dreaming of an England long gone, and to those from foreign climes with a romantic, picture postcard mental image of a Merrie England that probably never actually existed.

Nathan put the envelope to one side, and went off to make some tea. It was his unchanging habit to study any new script in a very precise and specific way. The place in which to digest and dissect the script was a luxurious, high-backed, all-embracing green buttoned leather wingback chair. This he had positioned right next to the large picture window that faced out over the grey, heaving, sullen swells of the North Sea. Equally vital to this first read through was a fortifying tray of tea and biscuits.

As he settled into the chair and placed the tray on the side table, the large, slightly out of breath form of Moriarty materialised. He had been at the far end of the garden intimidating a seagull when Nathan picked up the biscuit packet. The rustle of the plastic film encasing the biscuits, although faint, was detected, and he abandoned his psychological warfare with the seabird. Even from the distance of the garden gate he still managed to get to Nathan's side before the seal on the packet was fully breached.

Once the tray was ready with the accoutrements of the great English tea ceremony, and on this occasion, an opened packet of Ginger Nuts, Nathan settled down to review the script. Fishing out a small pocket knife he deftly sliced open the envelope, and slid out the script and covering letter. Reading through the letter he saw it contained a comprehensive list of rehearsal and shooting times, dates and locations. There was a second sheet stapled to it with a precis of his character and how he fitted into the overall plot. This he took some time to study.

The basic plot of this television epic revolved around a series of grisly murders that all occur in and around the village pub. This establishment is called The Moon, hence the title, "Evil Under the Moon." Somewhere in the writing department a writer was feeling smug, and indulging in a little personal back-slapping at managing to work in an allusion to one of Agatha Christie's novels, albeit with a slight twist to the title. The pub is located in the dead centre of town (pun intended). At opposite ends of the village are two antique shops (what else). These are run by two feuding brothers, each with their own little circle of friends and supporters. Such is their enmity that although related, they will stop at nothing to put each other out of business. Throughout the tale they indulge in a series of high jinks and low deeds. It becomes apparent through the telling of the story that they have a long-standing series of grievances with each other.

It probably hadn't occurred to the writers but the scenario as it stood was alarmingly similar to a Clint Eastwood spaghetti western called "A Fistful of Dollars." Had the writers noticed the resemblance, they wouldn't have been able to resist inserting some additional references into the narrative, just in case the viewers missed it. Authors love putting in subtle, and sometimes not so subtle nods to other works; it gives them an opportunity to show off and smirk privately about how well read and clever they are.

Nathan spent the next couple of hours carefully reading the script. In a small notebook he began to make notes about the character he was due to play, and the character he intended to play. He made this run through in one sitting, apart from a brief interlude to make another pot of tea. As Nathan read, sipped and munched, Moriarty sat contentedly consuming Ginger Nuts surrounded by a growing halo of crumbs.

Read through complete, Nathan laid the script aside and sat back in his chair. Placing his elbows on the armrests, he steepled his fingers and placed their tips against his chin. This pose was not essential for his meditation, but he was an actor, and as such he was always ever so slightly dramatic. Having gone over the plot in both outline and detail, he was more convinced than ever that he must have the other role. The part he was contracted to play was that of Sean Manderville. Of the two brothers he was the nasty one. Rude, bullying, misogynistic, arrogant, aggressive and manipulating. He wasn't the murderer of course. That would be far too obvious. Painting his character in shades of black was the writer's way of making him the main red herring. For a brief moment Nathan got mentally side-tracked trying to imagine a red herring in shades of black.

It is a standard plot device in dramas of this type to line up very obvious candidates for the murderer, while actually seeding little, subtle clues as to the identity of the real villain. If they do their job well, a fair percentage of the audience will be surprised at the final unveiling of the murderer. This will make them keen to watch the next story in the series, so they can see if they can work out who did it this time. Those who did correctly spot the guilty character will feel very pleased with themselves, and sit smugly telling their spouse, 'there you are, you see, I told you it was him.' They will also be sure to watch the next episode so they can show off again.

Getting his mind back onto the matter at hand he turned his attention to his rival in the story: Felix Manderville. The part of Felix was to be played by Dickie Valentin. Dickie was slightly older than Nathan, but much more well known. Some years ago, he had finished playing an unsavoury villainous pub landlord in a long running soap opera. His name, face and indeed persona were instantly recognisable to the television audience.

Since finishing his lengthy run in the soap, he had popped up in a variety of parts in multiple productions, all under the 'also starring' section of the cast list. From the audience's point of view, his was the famous face that would seem to be incongruously cast in a not quite big enough role. What it actually meant, was that he was the murderer. The give-away in so many of these stories is the 'spot the famous face' game. If you recognise a well-known face playing a minor character, you can be sure they will be pivotal to the solution. To try and deceive the television audience, the writers had created his character as the nice brother. In the story he was kind, polite, and in every respect the polar opposite of Nathan's scenery chewing, moustache twirling villainous character.

Dickie had fewer scenes than Nathan, though as a star he would be paid substantially more. What he did have though was the big end scene. As the murderer he had a very dramatic ending, complete with a final raging, manic piece of exposition. It is the finale where he gets to explain in great detail all the dastardly things he has done. This would be punctuated by a sequence of grainy flashback scenes, in which he is clearly seen for the first time as the murderer.

In this high-tension final scene, he would of course explain at length why the various characters he killed all had it coming. In this particular episode the ending included an exciting fight to the death with Detective Inspector Barrowboy on the burning roof of the suitably gothic manor house. All quaint English villages have an adjacent gothic manor house; it is a prerequisite of this type of drama. Across the inferno of the roof and battlements of the manor house, there are violent blows exchanged with our hero DI Barrowboy. The Detective Inspector, as is always the case in these stories, has ignored standard Police procedure and has completely failed to summon any back-up, and therefore must face the villain alone. After an epic battle, the homicidal maniac falls to a spectacular death.

Nathan's character of Sean Manderville had some good scenes, with some excellent over the top, moustache twirling villain lines. Nathan thought he could perform those well, and would be noticed in them, but they were as nothing compared to what he could do if he was playing the murderer. The finale was really good stand-out stuff. No, there was nothing for it, he needed to get that role. He could really spread himself with that part. The trick was how to achieve it. This wasn't like the stage productions he had hijacked before. He couldn't sabotage his fellow actor and step in as the understudy. Nobbling Dickie would simply mean the producers would just re-cast the part with another suitable well-known star. This time he needed to come up with a way to get the director or Dickie himself to want to swap the roles.

This would need careful thought. His biggest advantage was that actors all have one particular trait in common. They will all, on receipt of any script check it out thoroughly. This is to see how many lines they have, and whether their rivals have more or less lines than they do. They check who has the best scenes. Who can steal a scene. In short, they look for any opportunity to outshine and upstage each other. It was this ego driven obsession with the part and its size that he needed to play on.

If he could convince Dickie that his part was in some way inferior to Nathan's, then Dickie would himself be pressuring the Director to swap the roles. If Nathan could also apply pressure to the director on the same subject, then he felt he had a better than even chance of securing the part of the villain. As difficult as the mental games and poisoning of his previous sabotage efforts had been, this was a totally different venture. He needed a plan that would make Machiavelli look like an amateur.

19

POWER PLAY

Rehearsals began at the BBC studios in Norwich. The production company had secured a large open hall for the cast to work through the various scenes in the drama. Nathan and Moriarty arrived to find almost half the cast already assembled there. They clustered in small groups, chattering and cradling disposable cups of mass-produced coffee or tea. Harry Thorn, who played DI Barrowboy, spotted them as they came in and made a bee line for them. He was a familiar face and an old friend. They had worked with him on and off over the years, and he seemed very keen to renew their acquaintance.

He knew Moriarty well enough to scoop up a handful of biscuits from the refreshment table as he strode towards them. Moriarty had recognised him instantly and gave him a most affectionate greeting, especially as he came bearing consumable gifts.

Greetings concluded and biscuits consumed, Harry leant forward, and whispered in Nathan's ear.

'All I can say is I'm really not looking forward to this shoot,' he confided.

'Why ever not? You are the star of this show. I would have thought this was your best gig ever,' replied a puzzled Nathan.

'You'd think so wouldn't you,' he sighed. 'As you rightly say, this is undoubtedly the best part I've ever landed, and I have a five-year contract. No, my problem this time is that arrogant little snot Valentin. The director is already at his wit's end with him, and he only met him thirty minutes ago. Valentin is insisting on pretty comprehensive re-writes of his part. As he is the 'Guest Star' with emphasis on the word star, his agent is using his not inconsiderable clout to try and get the part rewritten the way Valentin wants it. Technically, I'm the star of the show, but he is doing his best to hijack the whole production. Unfortunately, as much as it's winding me up, it's you I really feel sorry for.'

'Me? What have I done?' Nathan's frown deepened.

He felt this rehearsal was taking a turn for the worse. Far from putting his plans into action, he began to feel as though an unseen current was sweeping him along.

Harry laughed a bitter chuckle.

'Valentin is a one trick pony. Every part he plays is a variation on his big soap role, a brooding, handsome rogue. He doesn't ever play nice characters. What he wants to do is meld your part as the villainous red herring character with his role as the murderer. This means he has basically removed almost every good scene you had, and taken it for himself. You are now the good, nice brother, but with dramatically less screen time. Though how that would make the audience think you are the murderer is beyond me.'

Nathan almost visibly rocked back on his heels. He quite simply hadn't seen this coming. He was so fixated on working out a way to eliminate Valentin, it had never occurred to him that Valentin would be trying to eliminate him. It seemed the hunter had become the hunted.

The sound of raised voices made them both turn and look to the far side of the hall as Valentin and the director squared off with each other and let rip with a full-on, no holds barred row. There followed a lot of arm waving, shouting, gesticulating, and on Valentin's part, energetic finger jabbing into the hapless director's chest. After some minutes of high energy disagreement Valentin threw his copy of the script into the red face of the director and stormed off. Passing Nathan and Harry he paused just long enough to shove his face into Nathan's visage. He was so close Nathan went slightly cross-eyed trying to keep him in focus.

'You Stockwood?' he growled.

'Yes, you must be Valentin.' He held out his hand in greeting.

This light hearted answer cut no ice with the angry actor. Snatching Nathan's copy of the script from his hand he tore it in two.

'You can forget that rubbish. Your part is being re-written. I will be telling you what scenes you get.'

Rehearsals continued throughout the week, though it was a far from happy process. The director stuck to his guns and insisted they rehearsed the script as it was written. Valentin on the other side of the trenches, argued every step of the way. He refused to do his scenes as written and would only perform the 'improved' scenes he and his agent were insisting on. Put simply, a stressful time was had by all.

For Nathan the entire process was unbelievably infuriating. For him, this time the shoe was on the other foot. Instead of controlling the situation, he was more or less powerless. He felt himself being squeezed out and he couldn't think of any way to stop it. Valentin, with greater star clout, and a much higher profile, all allied with a combative agent, held all the trump cards. Nathan had tried phoning his own agent, Trelawney Mancroft, who promised to do everything he could. By the following day he was told the only thing his agent had managed to achieve was a promise that he would still be paid as per the contract, even with his now dramatically reduced screen time. For Nathan that simply would not do. It wasn't about the money. He desperately needed to make an impression in this production. He needed to be noticed, to mark himself out as a star. The way it was going, he felt it would be a miracle if anyone even noticed he was in the show.

At the start of the first week of location shooting, Nathan and Moriarty drove to the Cambridgeshire village of Snelling. As he travelled, Nathan kept turning the problem round in his mind. No matter how hard he tried there seemed no solution to this conundrum. He felt a shudder run through him and his hands twitched on the steering wheel. Once again, the voice he had felt more than heard, whispered at the rear of his mind.

'It seems to me if you can't get the part, you can at least get even.'

That was it. If he couldn't save his own role in the drama, or get Valentin's part, he would at the very least find a way to exact some form of vengeance.

On the third day Nathan and Valentin were due to film one of the pivotal scenes in the drama. It was set on a small island on the lake of the adjacent Gothic mansion. In it the two brothers were supposed to have an intense verbal showdown.

Owing to the compact size of the location, access was restricted to just the actors and essential crew. They all had to be ferried across the lake, one by one, in a small rowing boat. Valentin had already made it loudly clear in no uncertain terms that he had to be taken across first. He was a star, and he wasn't going to twiddle his thumbs waiting for the lesser cast members. Nathan couldn't quite work out his logic as no filming could take place until both of them, plus the camera, sound and lighting crew were all present. In other words, it would be the same amount of time before the scene could be shot, whether he was first or last. Nathan assumed it was just another stage-managed grand gesture on Valentin's part to intimidate everyone around him.

With simple revenge as his goal, he set about putting his scheme into action. Once filming had finished the day before, instead of heading back to his van he headed for the lake. Locating the small wooden rowing boat, he spent a diligent hour working with a penknife, steadily loosening the bung in the bottom. Once he was happy it was pretty well hanging on by a wing and a prayer, he and Moriarty retired to their camper. If it all went according to plan, Valentin would be rowed across, and then either be stranded once the boat sank on its return journey, or joy of joys, be on the boat when it sank. A dunking in the cold waters of the lake should puncture his pompous attitude just a bit.

The morning was grey and overcast as Nathan and Moriarty watched the hunched, grumpy, surly figure of Valentin being ferried across the lake. His first qualm was when the boat got all the way back and was showing no sign whatsoever of sinking. The oars splashed, slapped and gurgled back, then halted alongside the wooden jetty. With some hesitation a nervous Nathan was ushered forward by the director. Standing on the jetty he looked intently at the scuppers. There was no sign of any leakage, not even the merest hint of dampness: the bottom of the boat was bone dry. In an attempt to move his sabotage on a pace, he stamped heavily as he clambered into the tiny craft. The boatman squawked in protest.

'Careful sir, you will have us both in the water,' he protested.

'Sorry, we don't want that do we,' Nathan mumbled unconvincingly.

As the man rowed, Nathan stared in mute frustration at the unmoving, recalcitrant bung.

After splashing ashore, he and Valentin stood in silent, mutual loathing on the shore and watched as the boat headed back to the far shore and the waiting film crew. At roughly the halfway point, the boatman seemed to have some kind of a fit. The boat rocked wildly as he thrashed about and then he burst into frenzied action, and started to row with exceptional vigour. It was sadly to no avail. He was still a good twenty feet from the jetty when the boat went under.

If the silence between Nathan and Valentin was awkward before, this quietude was worse. They both stared in shock as the reality sank in (rather like the boat). They were stranded, together. A few minutes later a squelching, complaining boatman hauled himself up onto the jetty. The drenched man flopped onto the wooden planks and yanked off his rubber boots, and poured a copious amount of water out of them.

They could just hear the director's voice calling to them faintly.

'Look, I'm really sorry about this, but we will have to leave you for a bit. I'm told there is another boat, but it is in the river some distance away. Don't worry we will be as quick as we can.'

The two stranded actors swapped a suitably horrified look, albeit for different reasons. It was with surprise that Nathan noticed Valentin's expression had become even more shocked, and was apparently directed just over his left shoulder. It was then he heard the hiss.

Turning, he came face to beak with what seemed to be the biggest swan he had ever seen. Just behind it was a second slightly smaller bird, presumably the female half of the assassination squad. For reasons that afterward Nathan was never able to ascertain, the presence of Valentin and himself was not welcome.

It was a quirk of Nathan's mind that it often strayed from the reality of the situation he was in. When faced with the unexpected, his thoughts went slightly sideways. He found himself thinking about a painting: Leda and the swan. It depicted the seduction of the titular Leda by Zeus, who for reasons probably best not thought about too deeply, materialised in fleshly form as a swan. The artist had painted a really big swan in an attempt to impress the divine origin of this particular bird on the viewer. All Nathan could think of at that moment was that the swan in front of him was, if such a thing was possible, even bigger. The swan then made its own feelings very clearly known, by raising itself up on tip toe, throwing out its chest and spreading its wings. It emitted a hiss like an incensed steam locomotive. Nathan carefully backed away. Unleashing a second louder hiss, it charged. Nathan turned and saw that Valentin was already disappearing around the bend in the shore. It is to his credit that he caught up to Valentin much quicker than he had expected.

The island was quite compact insofar as islands go. The two wheezing actors had only completed two laps before the second swan established the fact that she was female, and therefore decidedly brighter than her male companion. She achieved this by stopping, and running in the opposite direction. This meant that midway through lap three they were caught in an avian pincer movement.

Nathan screamed out.

'Head for the centre, there is a folly there, a sort of summerhouse thing.'

With Valentin hard behind him Nathan burst painfully through the clawing bushes. The summerhouse loomed into view. It was a marvel of totally impractical carpentry. In design it was circular, with a balustraded veranda, and a high peaked dome. The designer had clearly had a fascination with intricacy, as it had so much fretwork that it made the most ornate Swiss cuckoo clock look minimalist. Sadly however, as a protective structure it seemed to offer little or no practical protection for defending terrified actors from homicidal swans.

Leaping onto the balustrade Nathan wobbled precariously for a second.

'The roof, the roof,' he screamed.

While Nathan stood teetering trying to reach a suitable handhold, Valentin took advantage of his fellow actor's position and used him as an impromptu human ladder. Valentin propelled himself up Nathan's creaking back, shoulders, and as the last stepping stone, head. Once safely perched atop the ornate wooden roof, he made no attempt to help Nathan up to safety. A final ominous, extremely close hiss behind the struggling actor gave the required motivation for Nathan to take flight and clamber to safety. Nathan levitated upward, borne aloft on the twin wings of terror and adrenaline.

After some minutes had elapsed, and when they had both caught their breath, Nathan explained in exhaustive and minute detail just what he thought of Valentin. Valentin returned the favour by informing Nathan just how much he didn't care. The swans contented themselves going round the folly, and hissing in what Nathan considered a decidedly arrogant, self-satisfied manner. It was at that point they heard the first rumble of approaching thunder. The rain that followed was nothing short of Biblical.

After four hours the morose, drenched, shivering pair heard the sound of the director and the boatman calling their names and crashing through the undergrowth. The victorious swans turned to confront this new challenge to their domain. At the sight of their rescuers Nathan felt he could have wept with relief. The cold and the wet were trial enough, but this amount of time perched on the roof of the less than smooth surfaced folly, had lent a new and previously unknown meaning to the word fretwork. He had serious doubts that the nether portions of his body would ever feel the same again. As the rescuers came into sight the male swan gave his tiptoe, chest, wings and hiss routine an encore.

Charging toward the intruders the emboldened swan was horrified when the boatman thrust a large golfing umbrella in front of him and opened it with a decisive snap. The effect was astounding. In the swan's defence it has to be said that large colourful umbrellas were not part of their day-to-day life. If asked Nathan would have said it was impossible for a swan to do a back flip. This one managed it. The umbrella was opened and shut repeatedly in rapid succession, and the swans left the field of play.

By the time Nathan got back to Moriarty's welcome lean, he felt as if he had just been involved in an epic blend of Jurassic Park and The Flood. Shooting was suspended for the day as it was decided rain had stopped play.

20

HEAVY WEATHER

It was four days before either Nathan or Valentin had stopped coughing and wheezing. Finally, they felt well enough to resume shooting. The director however had made full use of that break in the filming. Without Valentin's constant haranguing he had been able to formulate a plan of his own. Having gone back to the producers of the show he had made it abundantly clear that unless Valentin was brought to heel, he would wreck the shoot. As the producers were first and foremost business men, the direct appeal to their wallets bore fruit. Having got their consent and full support, he emailed Valentin's agent.

As he laid it out there were only two options on the table.

One: Valentin played the part he was contracted to play with no further argument or diva tantrums,

Or:

Two: he could take Nathan's role and be the grumpy, but ultimately non-homicidal brother. This part would mean he could play to his strengths and be the villainous red herring in the story. However, if he chose this option, he must accept Moriarty as his faithful companion. This proviso was based on years of turning out this type of story. This meant he, the director, really knew his target audience.

It was primarily a middle class, middle of the road radio four type of audience. To a man, and woman, they were animal lovers. Anyone with an adorable scruffy wolfhound couldn't possibly be the murderer no matter how badly they behaved. It was pointed out to Valentin and his agent that the audience would never see the twist coming. He sweetened the deal with the suggestion that he would get rave reviews by being the first famous actor to appear in a murder series who wasn't the actual murderer.

Failure to agree to either of these options meant that the producers would just re cast his role.

After some deliberation, Valentin and his agent made a counter offer; a compromise between the two options. He would agree to swap roles with Nathan, but he could not appear with Moriarty under any circumstances. It seems he was allergic to dogs.

This compromise was accepted and Moriarty was instead cast with Nathan as the kind brother, who is in fact the twisted murderer. Moriarty was to take on the role of his faithful hound. Again, the same logic applied. How could anyone with an adorable dog be the murderer. After all everyone knows dogs are such good judges of character.

The filming progressed steadily. Scene after scene was completed and in the can. The chemistry between Nathan and Valentin had, for such a fanciful drama, acquired a strong realistic edge. You could almost believe they actually hated each other.

Nathan happily played the 'nice' brother and spent hours preparing for his big finish. The grand denouement with its fight to the death on the roof of a burning Manor House was nothing less than spectacular. After suitable rehearsing with the stunt team, Nathan felt extremely satisfied that he had performed the entire physical fight sequence himself, with the single exception of the final fatal fall from the roof. Moriarty stole every scene he was in. He shamelessly played to the camera and was the stand out performer of the entire show. This he considered was all perfectly correct and natural as everyone knew the world revolved around wolfhounds

Two months after the filming was completed the two companions sat in the Lord Nelson, sipping ale and in Moriarty's case, once again nibbling crisps. Nathan had done a lot of thinking in the days after the filming was complete. He had come to some uncomfortable conclusions. The main one was that he himself was completely useless. This realisation he found galling.

Three different productions. Three different roles pursued and achieved. However, something had occurred to him, something shocking. Each and every part had not been won by him. Yes, he had certainly made plans and laid stratagems. He had also spent hours putting them into operation. So, it came as something of a shock when he realised it wasn't his plans that had finally won the day.

Let's break them down.

Operation Poison LSD: On that caper he had first poisoned the wrong actor. He had successfully spiked the correct drink on his second attempt, but that still wasn't what brought about LSD's downfall. He never actually drank the laxative whisky. He just fell off the stage, and broke several bones. That fall was all as a result of Moriarty's impatiently pushing Deidre out of his way, and the human domino effect had come into play.

Operation Gaslight Sammy: In hindsight this was his most complex and carefully planned caper. Yet, at the end Sammy had seen though all the smoke and mirrors. All the high-tech wizardry and all the psychological tricks he had spent weeks putting into effect had all been for naught. Despite everything he had done, it was once again Moriarty as Black Shuck incarnate, looming unexpectedly from the shadows, that sent Sammy fleeing in terror. This was the reason Nathan could step into the role of Buttons.

Operation sabotage Valentin: This was perhaps the most embarrassing one of all. He actually had not had any feasible plan at all to replace Valentin. All he had was a scheme to exact a childish revenge, springing from what his mother would have called peevishness. Even that went spectacularly wrong. Again, what had tipped the scales? Why had he got the role? Valentin was allergic to Moriarty.

The more he thought about it, the inescapable fact that kept floating to the front of his conscious mind was that if he had done absolutely nothing, he would still have attained those roles. Plus, his conscience wouldn't have castigated him so much. The conscience was the second uncomfortable home truth. The extended, underhanded skulduggery he had carried out in his attempts to remove three otherwise competent actors from his career path, meant he had behaved in a less than honourable way. It took quite some time and meditation to square this behaviour with his conscience. As has been mentioned before he was in general a charming, affable, friendly man who was liked, possibly loved by his peers. Yet he had set about some pretty unpleasant scheming to get these poor unsuspecting performers out of his way. How on earth could he justify his actions?

Deep in his synapses his conscience was rejoicing in what seemed to be a return to civilised behaviour. His ambition however, was not out of the running yet. The counter-argument was vigorously deployed.

First Lancelot. There was an obvious need to supplant him in the starring role. The indisputable fact was that Nathan had chosen laxative poisoning as his method. This while unpleasant certainly wasn't fatal in any way. In addition, Lancelot was a financially successful actor, writer and director. Nathan taking the starring part had actually made the whole production both critically and financially more successful, thereby boosting

Lancelot's career. Lancelot was also an extremely pompous personality, and a little deflation of that rampant ego was not necessarily a bad thing. You could even call it a valuable life lesson. Nathan reasoned that this was suitable revenge for some of the dreadful plays Lancelot had written, and that he had sadly been a part of.

Secondly there was Sammy. Poor Sammy. This was the saga he felt most keenly. Sammy, like himself was an easy-going likeable man. Yet Nathan had carried out a dastardly scheme that had pushed an otherwise innocent man to the edge of madness. However, on the other side of the scales, Sammy was by no stretch of the imagination an actor. Especially not an actor who could carry the broad comedy of a panto. He would have come up short, and he would have known it. The audience would most definitely have known it. The whole panto would have been nothing more than a pale shadow of what it could have been. If you looked at it from the right direction, Nathan had saved Sammy from a humiliating failure and at the same time saved an otherwise doomed show.

Finally, we come to Valentin. That was probably the simplest of all. A pompous arrogant monster. He got everything he deserved. Although to be fair, having both been stuck on an island with rampant swans in the English monsoon, Nathan had shared fully in his misfortune. Even so, replacing him was not only just, it was frankly a delight.

So, conscience squared away, and his mind at ease he settled back in his seat. Looked at the right way, he had done nothing really sinful. Every action had a justifiable cause and indeed a good outcome. Added to which, each event moved him that little bit closer to his goal. The coveted part of O'Toole. When all was said and done, that was, and would remain his destiny.

Was there a lesson to be learned? Perhaps. He was certain he still felt that he really was destined to play that coveted part. He remembered the conversation he had all those weeks ago with Eric the landlord here in the pub. Right back when he first saw the notice about the O'Toole auditions.

'The thing about destiny is that it's destined.'

Was this true? If he just kept the goal in front of him and stopped trying to force the narrative, perhaps destiny would have its way.

He studied Moriarty carefully. Perched next to him on the settle surrounded by the heady aroma of pork scratchings and crisps he looked normal enough. Was this great, hairy, affable creature the instrument destiny was using to bring Nathan to that goal? Moriarty tool of the gods. He gave himself a mental shake. Stuff and nonsense. Put all that to one side and the one big inescapable truth was that in each role, once he was given the chance, he had excelled. That was solely down to him and his acting skills, his talent.

The two stage shows were both huge critical and financial hits. That would not have happened if he was no good in the leading role. Yes, his plans may have gone initially awry, yes Moriarty may have been the prime cause in their outworking. But it was Nathan's ability to channel the magic of O'Toole on stage and on camera that had allowed him to shine in these starring parts. His comedic genius as Buttons had stormed the stage in the panto. It had become the highest grossing panto the Theatre Royal had ever staged.

Tonight, the episode of Midwinter Homicides was to be aired. He felt nervous and uptight. Unlike a stage performance this was, 'In the Can,' so to speak. On stage he was not 'In the Can,' he was 'In the Moment.' With a live theatre audience each and every show was mutable: a thing he could shape and create. This television drama was done and dusted. What happened next was as much in the hands of the editing director as anyone. There was nothing more to do now except wait for the reaction. It was the performance equivalent of satellite communication, with an enormous delay. On stage you could feel the audience; their every breath told you how it was going. You could pick up the tempo, or slow it down, or even walk to the front of the stage and look them in the eye and break the fourth wall. But this was the actors' equivalent of the torture of Tantalus.

Taking a final sip from his glass and passing the last pork scratching to the expectant delicate jaws of Moriarty he stood up, and together they left for home. Hound and man in synchronous paced harmony. This evening he would sit, and watch with nervous trepidation the film performance he had worked so hard on. After that it was in the lap of the gods. Which would it be? Standout classic episode or just another forgettable midweek prime time drama? Sink or swim, this he felt was his last throw of the dice.

21
MAN OF LA MANCHA

Having sat through the midweek transmission of the murder mystery drama, Nathan was pleased with the end result. Even with his most critical hat on, he felt his performance was good. Not quite an O'Toole, but without a doubt, the closest he had ever come to it. The final showdown between him and the forces of law was the classical cliff-hanger ending. Despite the mediocrity of the plot, and the cheesy dialogue, he had managed to tap into the essence of O'Toole. He had managed to rise above the material. In the final scene he attacked his lines with malevolent menace, and strutted with a barely contained evil. He drove his co-star into the background with the sheer vitality of his performance.

Many of these murder shows could often stray into a form of muddy panto. Cliched characters going through the familiar tropes in idyllic bucolic settings. They ambled along inviting the lethargic, sofa reclining viewer to unpick the clues and sift out the red herrings, in between rushing to make tea in the commercial breaks. The murders were free of gore or of any real violence, but were always touched with that twist of English eccentricity which could trace its roots back to John Steed and Emma Peel. This time however, the story was raised above its fellows. The combination of the famous face not being the murderer and Nathan's powerful, driving performance took it to a new level. It just remained for the audience to pass their judgement.

Two days later Nathan got a call from his agent.

'I really think you've cracked it this time. That episode of Midwinter Homicides has become the watercooler moment of the year.'

The expression "watercooler moment" momentarily perplexed Nathan. He tended to let many modern idioms pass him by, as befitted a man who tended to dwell a decade or two behind the rest of the world.

'Is that a good thing?' he queried.

'Good, it's absolutely brilliant. My phone is ringing off the hook with job offers for you. Admittedly many are for the type of work you usually do, but now more than half are actual starring parts. You've done it. You are a star in the making.'

'Yes, but is it enough?' queried Nathan. 'Will it get me in the audition room for the O'Toole biopic?' Even more importantly if I get in, what are my chances? I need to be sure I've got a fighting chance in there.'

'I won't kid you Nathan, you would probably get into the audition, no problem. What your chances are once you are there though is another matter entirely. I know for a fact that two of your recent rivals are definitely going for it.'

Nathan paused. He dreaded the answer, but he had to ask.

'Who?'

'Lancelot and Valentin. They both want the part pretty badly, and are considered fairly highly, if not up there as front runners. Their agents both seem to think they are in with a good chance.'

Nathan quietly and after a few seconds said with infinite fragile dignity,

'Just a moment.'

Pressing the mute button on the handset he carefully placed the phone down on the table, walked out the patio doors and gave a primal scream with distinct echoes of Johnny Weismuller's Tarzan yell. Seagulls took off in a great cloud, two children dropped their ice creams, Moriarty surged to his feet in a passable impression of a vertical take-off jet and galloped to Nathan's side. He had been sprawled belly up in a sunny spot just inside the apartment and had been in the middle of a wonderful dream in which he had chased, and caught the biggest steak pie he had ever seen. Now, panting and flustered he looked around, and seeing no danger whatsoever he gave Nathan a look of extreme disappointment. Muttering under his breath, he wandered back to the warm spot where he had been enjoying the sun shining in through the window. There were times he thought, when, as much as he loved Nathan, the whole faithful hound protecting his master routine was tested just a bit too far.

Retrieving the telephone Nathan unmuted it and calmly said,

'Really, what a surprise.'

Despite the well-mannered reply the actor's agitation was obvious. Trelawney's smooth voice tried to calm him.

'I know that wasn't what you wanted to hear but you must be realistic, you should have known there will be a lot of competition for this role. On the plus side I've got some extra good news that will definitely boost your standing, and raise your profile with the casting directors.'

'It can't be another acting job there isn't time. The auditions start in just a couple of months.'

'No, no. Not an acting job. Better than an acting job. Brace yourself. An interview on The Perkinson show.'

Nathan was momentarily speechless. Not a normal situation for an actor.

'How? Why? More to the point, why me? He is the number one celebrity interviewer. He only does the top stars.' The words tumbled out of him in a confused rush.

'Ordinarily yes you would be correct. He doesn't stoop to the level of dealing with humble newly rising stars like yourself, but this show is a special. He has a selection of writers, directors, rising new actors, and older performers like yourself. They have all been chosen to explore where today's theatre and the film industry is going. It will be called "Perkinson Explores the Future of Showbusiness." There is a new writer who has an experimental piece on the dynamics of gender politics, that's currently on in the West End. Then they've prised old Prassburger out of his retirement home as an example of classic British cinema direction. A new teen actress who is doing a play on the green activist, that's the Greta Thimble story. Plus, you. You are there as an example of Popular British theatre and TV. The old guard if you like. The fact that you are currently flavour of the month after the last three things you've done helped me get you onto the show.'

Nathan paused while a huge grin slowly crept across his face.

'If I could weave in my goal of playing O'Toole in the upcoming film.' he said. 'It could help prime the pump with the casting directors. It certainly wouldn't hurt my chances. Thank you. I will need you to swing it so I can bring Moriarty in with me.'

'That's already arranged, he has been assigned a visitor pass for the studio,' answered Trelawney.

'I explained all about the way you two go everywhere together and they actually want him to be there. They may even bring him into the interview. Apparently, he adds to your eccentric thespian charm, which amazingly, is something they think is a good thing. All I can say is they obviously haven't met you two.'

The conversation wound down to a few back-and-forth comments, and mutual congratulations. Nathan eventually hung up the phone and wandered out into the garden. Gazing off into the distant North Sea horizon, he slowly paced to the end of the lawn. Hands in pockets, a half-smile on his face. For the first time in months, he felt content.

When, like a latter day, less geriatric Don Quixote, he had started this quest, he had seen nothing but windmill giants at which to tilt. Pitting his puny frame and puny fame against other more famous actors. However, against all the odds he had won through. A star in three consecutive productions and now going to be interviewed by the king of the celebrity interviews himself, Michael Perkinson. He had wasted years he thought, in meandering along as a comfortable jobbing actor. Now he had unleashed his inner O'Toole. That potential had always been there. He had it at the start of his career, but had lost it somehow along the way. Now it was back, and it was burning inside him. Like his idol he was hungry. He could almost feel O'Toole's presence, standing just behind him. He would never be second best again. When he performed, he wanted to blow everyone else out of the water. In any scene, all the audience would see would be him. All they would remember would be him, and his performance.

Moriarty, who had given up trying to recapture his best dream of all time, sauntered over to see what it was that Nathan was staring at. Wolfhounds after all must never be kept out of anything. He stood next to Nathan and peered over the low stone wall. He looked left, he looked right, he looked straight ahead: nothing. Perplexed he looked up at Nathan. He tried to work out Nathan's eyeline, then did his best to copy it. Still nothing, just sun, sky, sea and seagulls. Nathan wasn't even looking at the only remotely amusing sight in view. This was a rugby scrum of seagulls fighting over two dropped ice creams, while a pair of children were hauled snivelling and protesting away in opposite directions by their respective parents.

Moriarty pondered the changes that were happening in his friend and companion. For the last few years, the pair had gently wandered through life together. Happy, content and unambitious. Now he could see a marked difference in Nathan. He could even smell it. The chemicals that course through our bodies all have their own unique aroma. To the sensitive nose of Moriarty, they were now starting to shout 'Alpha male.' On top of that were the exceptionally intense shifts. These were brief and only happened occasionally, but they were powerful. When they struck, Nathan underwent a strong, dramatic transformation. Moriarty could not pin down just what was happening to his brother, but the elevation in his confidence and status went sky-high. Although puzzled by the changes he didn't really mind them. Wolfhounds take life as it comes. He had to admit that the last few months had been considerably more incident filled, and as a result much more entertaining. Not that their previous routine had been entirely free from excitement.

There was the accidentally knocking the jogger into the sea incident. The time all those other dogs followed him home, and the complaints of their owners. The falling in the scummy dyke, twice: with its inevitable hosing down. The mysterious affair of the stolen coconut cake. He actually thought he was unlucky to be blamed for that, even though he was definitely guilty. The splitting of the tip of his tail in overexcited wagging, and subsequently turning the hallway into a passable murder scene with the blood splatters. Walking down the hall just after Nathan had laid terracotta tiles to enrich the appearance of the entrance, resulting in the cement drying and leaving of a trail of randomly spaced wonky tiles in an otherwise perfectly level floor. One for each weighty step of a wolfhound. He remembered there had been a lot of shouting about that particular incident.

Then there was the designer silk cushion debacle. In his defence he was just a teenager at the time, and he had been very bored. Yes, he did take the cushion outside. Yes, he did play with it. Yes, it did explode. Yes, it was full of feathers. Sadly, that was the point at which Nathan came out and found him looking like a cross between a wolfhound and a goose. When Nathan attempted to clear the feathers off the lawn, he learnt that sweeping and even raking a lawn covered in goose feathers does not work very well. As a result, both the holiday makers progressing along the Southwold promenade, that ran along outside their apartment, and the immediate neighbours, were treated to the sight of Nathan vacuuming the lawn. This went down in town folklore as an example of just how hard the residents worked to retain their perfect picture postcard appearance.

Not to mention all the different journeys the length and breadth of the country from theatre to playhouse, and the plethora of eccentric thespians they had met. Yes, they had a number of adventures and events to look back on, but the last few months had been an absolute rollercoaster. People had fallen over, dived off stage, been poisoned, had screaming fits. There had been chases, fainting, even invisible dogs. He had even watched from a great distance as Nathan was locked in mortal combat with a giant white bird. But most intriguing of all was Nathan's transformation from contented Beta to hungry, thrusting Alpha.

He found himself looking forward to what was coming next.

22

VENUS

The show was being filmed in the BBC studios in Salford. The titular star, Michael Perkinson, was a bluff straight-talking northerner and vociferously proud of that fact. He also ticked the cliché box by being strongly disparaging of the south. As a result, he preferred to film on his home soil. Nathan and Moriarty travelled up several days early, and spent a relaxing time exploring the area and carrying out an intensive survey of the local ales and cuisine. Moriarty gave the local chips a five-star rating.

They arrived early at the studios and parked in the nearest car park, the van only just fitting under the height restriction barrier. Many modern car parks deployed this tactic to deter the larger vehicle. On more than one occasion Nathan had let the air out of his tyres to allow him to squeeze under. He carried an electric pump for the express purpose of reinflating them afterwards. Though never a boy scout he heartily embraced the motto, "Be Prepared."

Before they set out, Moriarty had submitted to the unpleasantness of a bath. Brushing he hated, baths he would tolerate. Given his upcoming appearance Nathan wanted him to look and smell at least semi-presentable. Owing to his size the sink and the bath were definitely not possible. It was the garden hose on the patio and a brisk rub down with towels. Having completed the washing stage, Moriarty implemented his own post wash routine of a good shake or two followed by a vigorous roll on the lawn, thereby bringing him back to almost the same state he was in before the cleansing effects of the bath.

They entered the modern glass and steel edifice of the BBC Media Centre and presented themselves at the front desk. Here after the usual amazement at Moriarty and his vast size they signed in, and were each equipped with an identifying lanyard, to be hung around their necks emblazoned with the word 'Visitor.' They were given directions to the second floor where they were to go to conference room one for a pre interview briefing. Nathan decided they would take the stairs.

As has been mentioned previously in this tale, using the stairs has its drawbacks. Moriarty lined himself up on the first set. Taking a deep breath, he commenced his run up. Claws clattering, he propelled himself upwards gathering speed and momentum. The stairs curved upwards in a spiral. This meant luckless staff ascending and descending past the curve got quite a start. One unfortunate man caught horribly unawares by this vast furry monster charging up towards him, squealed in horror and grabbed the young lady next to him to use as a human shield. Nathan trotted up after him throwing apologies left and right as they shouldered past.

They paused on the first-floor landing. Partly to catch their breath, and partly to assess the damage left in Moriarty's wake. Fortunately, this was so far fairly minimal, just a few startled office staff.

They lined up on the second set of stairs. Sadly, at this point Nathan was distracted by a passing man who asked one of the many inevitable questions about Moriarty. As a result, he was left behind as Moriarty commenced his next ascent. Extracting himself as quickly and politely as he could, he discovered Moriarty had already disappeared round the curve. There was a high-pitched scream, and a great pile of paper came fluttering round the bend. It spread itself out like giant rectangular snowflakes across the steps. Sprinting upwards, he found Moriarty halfway up the next section of stairs bending solicitously over a prostrate man who, white faced and trembling, was uttering an unending appeal to his deity of choice. Gently nudging Moriarty to one side, Nathan helped the shocked man to his feet and set about picking up the scattered papers. An unexpected Moriarty can have that effect.

Arriving at the conference room they found they were the last to arrive. Entering the bland corporate room, they met the other interviewees. Introductions were made, hands were shaken, Moriarty was made a fuss of. Arranging themselves around the table, the producer handed each of them a slim folder with the briefing notes. He then sat down next to Michael Perkinson.

The show's producer Dermot de Havilland cleared his throat and began.

'Right, well, I will just go over the basics and then you can retire to the green room, or your dressing rooms to go over the notes in your own time. Filming will commence in Studio A1 at two this afternoon. There is a restaurant on this floor for you to use, at the BBC's expense of course. In essence what we want is your opinions on the current and future state of the entertainment industry. You all have very different views and backgrounds so we will expect a lively discussion. Michael has some good strong questions for you, the gist of which is in your notes. Please feel free to express yourselves as honestly as you like. If you don't agree with each other that's fine, in fact so much the better. A little conflict always makes for great television.'

Tristram Candy, director of the new wave, weighed in straight away. His face set and determined.

'My view is clear and simple. The productions of the past are exactly that. The past. They have no relevance to the truly important theatre and film we are producing now.'

He sat back in his chair face firm and resolute, arms folded, daring anyone to challenge him.

Emmerich Prassberger immediately bristled.

'You arrogant jumped-up little man. The reality is that your pygmy productions stand on the shoulders of giants. We told real stories about real people. We had narratives that spoke to real individuals with real lives. Not the whining of a disaffected generation of spoilt, self-important brats that strut and whine on about how hard done to they are. Try living through a world war. Then you can talk.'

Esme, the young actress looked like a rabbit caught in the headlights. She was clearly a personality that was not happy with conflict. Face red with suppressed emotion she spoke.

'I can't speak for the rest of you, but the work I'm doing is about issues that have an impact on everyone. No planet, no people.'

Nathan watched slightly stunned by the level of confrontation around the table. If it was like this now, what would happen when the cameras were rolling?

He gave a small cough to announce himself.

'I just think every single one of us are artists in our own right. We all contribute something that is quite simply unique to us. I'm not sure we should be competing.'

Michael Perkinson, who had up till now been smiling, probably in anticipation of a hotly contested programme that would be popular with his audience, frowned. The last thing he wanted was a peacemaker in his panel of opposing views. Rodney Haviland, plastered on an unconvincing weak smile and tried to settle the mood in the room.

'Well, we all have our points of view of course. Look, let's break up now and go through our notes and then we can come back into the studio for a good lively discussion.'

More like a good lively fight thought Nathan.

One hour before filming was due to commence a timorous knock on the door of Nathan's dressing room announced the arrival of the makeup people. Three petite young women hovered nervously in the doorway.

'Hello. We know we look a bit mob handed but the producer wanted your lovely dog to have a bit of a tidy up, and a brush before filming the show.'

Hearing the dreaded word 'brush' Moriarty surged up onto his feet, eyes wide in shock. An astute Nathan, wise to his hound's dislike of grooming, shot out a hand and grasped Moriarty's collar before he could make a swift exit. Moriarty looked up at him with an accusing eye. "Et tu, Brute" he thought.

With Nathan's firm grip on his collar, the three girls set to work. En-masse they were able to get the job done in record time, while Moriarty stood in stiff legged horror at this torture. Sticky straggly bits of unknown origin and provenance were trimmed away, knots of matted fur were delicately teased out and unravelled. The shaggy monster of Baskerville Hall was rapidly transformed into a gleaming giant of Crufts like quality. Work done, the three paused to take some selfies of themselves with the new sleek Moriarty. This fussing restored some of his good humour, and now the look he gave Nathan was not so much withering, but more one of resigned disappointment.

Only a little while later, an intern came and called them to the studio. Moriarty sat to one side as Nathan was equipped with a discreet microphone and ushered to his seat on the brightly lit dais ringed by a semicircle of cameras. Behind the cameras was a rising bank of tiered seating. Filling this was a murmuring and whispering crowd of around three hundred people. Tonight's eager audience, all in for a free evening's entertainment.

Nathan was sat next to Michael Perkinson who took the centre seat. On his left the young actor Esme Cannon sat fidgeting with nervousness. She leaned in and whispered conspiratorially,

'I've never done anything like this before. I don't believe how stressed it's got me.'

'Me to,' replied Nathan in an undertone. 'I think as actors we are more comfortable with a script. It's so much easier just repeating someone else's words. Having to speak for myself is a new experience.'

To Perkinson's right the two directors, old and young were ignoring each other with a palpable disdain that seemed to lower the temperature around them. A few last-minute instructions were issued by the director, then he retired to the glass screened control room that hung on the back wall over the audience. The main lights went down, and the dais stood out in a glittering oasis of light. The audience went quiet. The stage manager counted them in from five to one and the introductory music began.

As the show got under way Perkinson masterfully showed why he was the country's premier interviewer. He skilfully kept the conversation flowing without allowing the disagreements to break into outright warfare. His public persona was that of the straight-talking bluff, no nonsense northerner. A man who had pulled himself up by his bootstraps. In all respects a professional Yorkshireman. This simple, everyman front, meant people often underestimated him. He threw in unexpected curve ball questions in addition to those listed in the pre-show notes. This kept the discussion moving, but with just enough verbal battling to make it good entertainment for the audience.

From the outset, it was obvious the two directors just couldn't agree on anything. Tristram dismissed all directorial work, film and theatre more than five years old as dated and pointless garbage that should be consigned to the bin of history. Emmerich took this as a personal attack on his own work. Creations that he considered as part of the classical heritage of British cinema. Frankly most reviewers and historians of British cinema would have agreed with him on that view. In their time his films were as cutting edge and ground-breaking as Tristram's work was considered to be now.

It was clear to Nathan that the real root of their mutual loathing was simply that they were from different eras. They had widely opposite world views, and would never really agree on anything. Perkinson played on that. He asked leading questions that nudged one, then the other, into dogmatic assertions that the other director would automatically disagree with.

Unhappy with any kind of conflict Esme tried vainly to calm this escalating war.

'Surely, it's about the work we are all doing now, and have done in the past. It was all good in its time, but time and public tastes change. I'm a prime example of that. I only do modern, relevant work. I actually struggle to follow the type of English used in older work. Shakespeare for example. I've read it many times, but I just can't understand what it is trying to say.'

Here Nathan felt was a subject on which he could finally contribute. Up till now he had said nothing, he had just allowed the rancorous debate to wash over him.

'That is because Shakespeare isn't meant to be read. It's meant to be spoken aloud. Only then do you get the rhythm of the prose,' he explained.

Tristram snorted. 'Rubbish, outdated drivel is all Shakespeare is.'

Emmerich rose to the bait. 'What would you know? As I understand it you haven't actually written anything, not a single line. You just get your actors to improvise.'

Before the fight could get fully under way, Perkinson stepped in and changed the direction back to Nathan.

'You raise an interesting point there Nathan. I understand you are actively pursuing the role of Peter O'Toole in an upcoming film of his life and career. He is an excellent example of an acting tradition that runs from the films of Emmerich here, through to stars like O'Toole and Burton. From them it goes onto actors such as yourself who are the current crop of older well-established performers, and continues on to the new wave, such as Tristram and Esme. Can I ask you, are the great performances of classic theatre and film by people like O'Toole still relevant now?'

Nathan took a deep breath. He felt as though every spotlight was on him, which in a way it was. This was his chance to not only defend his work, but that of the actor he wanted to be.

'Well, the thing is not very easy to lay out simply. The nub of it lies in defining what we mean by relevant. Perhaps I could explain by using Esme's difficulty with Shakespeare as an example.'

'As I say, you have to perform it to understand it. I'm not denigrating Tristam's or Esme's work, but like much of the newer stuff, it tends to break itself up into smaller and smaller audiences. It addresses specific, almost niche problems. Gender issues, climate problems, racism, sexism.'

He could see Tristram drawing a deep breath and preparing to leap into the fray. He quickly finished his train of thought. He had to get his point across.

'They are all worthy and important subjects, but they are divided into bite size topics for a select audience. Shakespeare wrote about the wider issues of life; he wrote about people. All people. Irrespective of their race, gender, sex or class. People who had the same fears, loves, hates, worries and challenges we do right now. That is why his writing is not just beautiful, it's still relevant worldwide.'

'Actors like O'Toole got that. They didn't just act a part. They lived their roles. O'Toole inhabited, and literally breathed life and reality into his characters. His portrayals were of such power they totally entranced his audiences. He was probably the greatest actor of his generation.'

Emmerich butted in. 'Of any generation if you ask me. I saw him on stage several times back in the day. I have never seen anyone act with such clarity and intensity. The way he held an audience was magical.'

Nathan was warming to his subject now. 'Exactly. You know every morning he would get up and go outside into his garden and recite Shakespeare sonnets to the birds. He knew the texts inside out. He was like that with every performance he gave. The hours of practice he put in before rehearsals was phenomenal. That is why neither Shakespeare or O'Toole's performances will ever go out of date.'

He sat back feeling a little drained and surprised at himself for such a passionate speech.

Michael Perkinson gave a little half smile. Raising his voice, he threw down the gauntlet.

'Well, as I hear you are trying to get to play him in an upcoming film of his life and career, and you have given us such a spirited defence of both him and Shakespeare, I think we should get you to prove it. Show us why they are so good. Give us an example.'

Nathan wished the ground would swallow him up. Him and his big mouth. Now what could he do?

It was then, in that moment of uncertainty that he once again heard that familiar, quiet voice. A shiver ran through him. Afterwards, he could never be sure if the voice was in his head, or from just behind him. It was however a voice he knew better than he knew his own. Clear and precise he heard the slow, slightly breathy drawl of O'Toole.

'Don't worry old sport. Just leave this to me.'

Behind the camera Moriarty sat up. The fur on his back and neck bristled upright. He shivered slightly, although it was far from cold. The change was happening to Nathan again, and this time it was more powerful and profound than it had ever been before. He couldn't describe it, but it was a huge transformation. There was a distinct shift in his entire body energy. If it were not for his scent, which Moriarty could still clearly pick up, he would almost swear Nathan was someone else entirely.

To the astonishment of the others on the dais, and to the audience, a subtle but very definite change came over Nathan Stockwood. His entire body shifted and morphed slightly. He suddenly seemed just that little bit taller, and that little bit thinner. His posture altered.

He slid forward until he was sitting on the very edge of his seat. Leaning towards Esme he placed his elbows on his knees, his head bowed and in shadow from the spotlights. Reaching out his left hand he took hold of her slim fingered right.

Still with his head bowed he spoke.

'I need to set the scene. This is from an O'Toole film called "Venus." In it he plays an aging actor called Maurice, who falls in love with a much younger woman. In some ways it could be seen as inappropriate, creepy even. Especially in this "hashtag me too" era. But such is his, and the other actor's performance in this film it is anything but creepy. It is quite simply beautiful.'

'In this scene the young woman is taking a bath in his apartment. He is sat in the next room. The door between them is shut. She tells him a deeply personal story about how the people she loved and trusted betrayed her, abused her. This heart-rending tale moves him so deeply he feels an irrepressible urge to give her some crumb of comfort, but he doesn't have the words. How can you talk away such searing sorrow and pain. So, he does what every actor would do. He uses someone else's words. He gets up and standing with his cheek against the closed door of the bathroom he recites Sonnet 18.'

Nathan sat holding the young actor's hand, head down, staring at his feet. He felt the change come over him. All the years of studying O'Toole. All the hours spent watching his performances. All the notebooks he had filled with details of posture, inflection, pace, tone and delivery came together into one magical moment. He lifted his head and looked straight into her eyes. She actually gasped. He looked different. Whether it was the overhead spots or the utter immersion into the character, but he looked like O'Toole. The cheekbones seemed just a touch higher and clearer cut, the face was longer. But mostly it was the eyes. They were blue, but not their previous blue. These eyes shone, they glowed with an inner light that seemed to pin her to her chair. But all of that was as nothing compared to the voice.

To those who heard it, the effect was mesmerising. It flowed into their ears, and connected with some inner kernel of understanding in their minds. A secret, hitherto unknown cluster of brain cells that knew and recognised absolute truth. To Nathan it was a blend of both his own voice, and the inner recording of that scene as it played out in his mind. His voice and O'Toole's matched, synchronised, and mixed in perfect harmony. Beat for beat, tone for tone. Every pause, every little inflection matched with his memory of the scene.

'Shall I compare thee to a summer's day?' *The line rising rapidly in tone and pitch to throw the question without raising his voice.*

'Thou art more lovely and more temperate.' *The pitch a shade deeper, the words slightly clearer and more defined.*

'Rough winds do shake the darling buds of May

And summers lease has all too short a date.' *Faster, setting the rhythm to punch the words while leaving them clear and concise.*

'Sometimes too hot the eye of heaven shines

And often is his gold complexion dimmed.' *Slower, a wistful sad note creeps in.*

'And every fair from fair sometimes declines.' *Draw out the sorrow of this truth, leave a minute pause between each word.*

'By chance or nature's changing course untrimmed.' *Delivered with a verbal shrug, a truth that cannot be changed but can only be accepted and endured.*

'But thy eternal summer shall not fade.' *Powerful. Each word hit with enough top spin to land in the audience with steely strength and conviction.*

'Nor lose the possession of that fair thou ow'st

Nor shall death brag thou wander'st in his shade.' *Punch this. Defiant, strong.*

'When in eternal lines to time thou grow'st.' *Appealing, reassuring, encouraging. Then big pause. Final lines drawn out and launched with all his skill and power.*

'So long as men can breathe or eyes can see

So long lives this, and this gives life to thee.'

The moment hung in the air. A suspended second of infinite length. A crystallised gem of frozen time. Utter silence. It seemed the entire room was holding its breath. The young actor sat motionless. Her mouth slightly open in shock at the power of what had just happened. From the lidded walls of her eye, one single tear broke free and rolled down her perfect, youthful cheek. Unheeded, unwiped, un-mourned. She placed her free hand over Nathan's.

'I never…. I didn't…. I had no idea it could be like that,' she whispered.

Her unfinished sentences seemed to float in the air. With one movement the entire audience surged to their feet. They clapped. They clapped as they had never applauded before.

On the dais the other participants also stood. The noise was an overwhelming, buffeting, roaring wave of sound.

At that perfect point, with the impeccable timing of the world's greatest scene stealer, Moriarty stood up. He gave a shake to straighten his glistening coat, and with all his awesome majesty, strode towards Nathan. He entered the spot-lit stage area with measured stately strides, his head high and proud, his freshly groomed pelt glowing. Mounting the dais, he turned and sat next to Nathan. He considered the now openly weeping Esme. His head cocked gently to one side as he gave her his deepest, most profound, understanding stare. A look of such grace and benediction, that it captured all her attention. He then raised one massive paw and gently laid it on her knee. In recognition of a great Irish actor, sat a great Irish wolfhound.

The crowd went wild. They didn't just clap now, they whistled, they roared, they shouted and they stamped. Nathan leant forward and just loudly enough for the microphones to register it he said,

'That is the timeless power of Shakespeare, delivered with the spellbinding magic of O'Toole.'

High in the control room the director, in an echo of Nathan, leant forward over the sound technician's shoulder, and placed a trembling hand on her back.

'Please tell me you got all that? Because that right there, boys and girls is our award-winning moment of the year.'

23
GREAT CATHERINE

Moriarty gave a long stretch on the sofa that served as his bed in the kitchen of his and Nathan's apartment, rolled off, and stood up. He gave himself a good shake to correctly align the still far too brushed and groomed coat, and considered starting his supervisory role. His first task as always was to wake Nathan. It was with wistful regret that he considered Nathan was far too prone to lay in and sleep, when there was clearly so much that needed to be done. His friend he recognised sadly, had a well pronounced lazy streak.

He quietly padded into the darkened bedroom and considered what method to use today. The tongue lathered across the cheek? The cold wet nose in the ear? Perhaps the gentle paw dropped with a resounding thud on the chest? No, he thought, after their magnificent success yesterday, in which he considered he took the lion's or more accurately wolfhound's share, he decided use an old favourite.

As gently as possible he climbed onto the bed next to Nathan. His friend was a fairly deep sleeper, but even so caution must be taken. Arranging himself carefully he laid his great chest across Nathan's ribs. All was still for a precious, peaceful moment, then Nathan began to pant, then gurgle in a breathless wheeze. Gasping and blue-faced he erupted from beneath the weighty bulk of Moriarty. He surged from the duvet coughing and using words of great passion. Moriarty lay watching the now deeply breathing Nathan, and smiled inside. If a job is worth doing it is worth doing well.

Although it was now time to take Nathan out for his early morning walk, Moriarty decided to wait before imparting this reminder. He knew from long experience that any attempt to go out before Nathan had consumed at least one cup of tea, was not only doomed to failure, but usually led to complaints and a bit of an atmosphere. Instead, he ambled to the patio doors and stood staring intently at them. Eventually a darkly muttering Nathan tottered over and opened them. Exiting for a lap of the garden and the strategic placement of his unique territory odour markers, he left Nathan to feed his tea addiction.

Returning some ten minutes later, he began to communicate to the now dressed Nathan, that it was his walk time. Although not being able to speak English, the combination of the correct gestures, hops and barks got the point across. In this case it was the 'play bow' placing both front paws together and stretching forward, head down, hips up. Then standing up straight, a little hop and a short huff of a bark. Like most dogs Moriarty was convinced Nathan understood every word he said.

Gathering up the lead and a roll of small bags Nathan and Moriarty headed out to the promenade and the beach. The two friends ambled along the promenade and down to the beach. Although still early there was the usual selection pack of other locals and dogs, plus a smattering of early summer visitors. This meant the walk was punctuated by the familiar pauses while various people stopped and expressed their wonderment at his magnificence. There were even a few of the inevitable requests for photographs with him. He accepted this adoration as the perfectly normal thing it was. Sometimes though he felt a little sorry for Nathan. No one ever wanted to take his picture. He considered it a sterling example of good character that this never seemed to bother his companion. In fact, it seemed to Moriarty that Nathan enjoyed basking in the reflected glory.

Despite these interruptions and Moriarty's dutiful checking and updating of the various odour messages and markers left by other local residents, he found his mind was not really on the subject of the walk. He was instead meditating on the change in Nathan. Dogs possess all the same senses as other sentient beings, but for them smell takes centre stage. It hogs the limelight, and provides vast amounts of information to the canine brain.

For almost the entirety of their relationship Nathan's smell had radiated contentment. The pair had ambled through a life that was happy, calm and relaxed. In the last nine months however, that had undergone a radical change. Moriarty felt it all seemed to start when Nathan had overindulged last year at the Lord Nelson. Since then, Nathan's odour profile was more of a rollercoaster ride. Despair, elation, fear, anger, disappointment, joy, victory, stress, determination. The list of olfactory messages he had been exuding seemed almost endless. Now, after the events of last night, he had a new aroma to add to the list: quiet determined ambition. He was displaying all the signs of someone taking on the mantle of a pack alpha. He was supremely confident.

In addition, there were all the other events that had taken place recently. The gentle unhurried rhythm of their life together had taken on a much more dramatic and, on occasions comical aspect. Moriarty didn't mind this. It was, if nothing else engaging. He just worried where it was all going to lead to.

Returning home, he immediately started the communication process that reminded Nathan it was time for breakfast. There was a slight confusion over the status implications of this. Dog etiquette dictated that the pack alpha provided the food for the pack. Nathan certainly did that. However, the same etiquette expected the pack alpha to eat first, and Moriarty ate first. This made them two alphas in a pack of two. Moriarty squared this circle in his own mind by making them equal alpha. Although it must be acknowledged that he of course was more equal than Nathan.

Cooked chicken was placed in his bowl and mixer added and stirred in. It frustrated him that Nathan kept putting that stuff in his food. He completely understood that it was supposed to be good for him, but it wasn't anywhere near as tasty as the chicken. Still, if he used his tongue and snout properly, he could shove a lot of it to the side of the bowl and uncover the meat. As he munched, he was dimly aware that Nathan went off to answer the phone.

Stomach full, appetite satisfied, he ambled outside to assume his 'lie on the lawn and remind the seagulls that this is my space' pose. You had to work hard to stay on top of seagulls or they got above themselves. He was disturbed in this vital task by Nathan performing an impromptu jig and singing his way out onto the patio. Cavorting around Moriarty in a most undignified and sadly out of rhythm way he declared,

'Come on Puss we are going to London, and I won't become Mayor but I will become Peter.'

'Puss.' The cheek of the man. They were great and loyal friends but he was not, and never would be a cat.

Before the kettle had boiled, Nathan picked up the silent, psychic message that Moriarty wanted to go into the garden. This phenomenon was something all wolfhound owners experienced with alarming regularity. When your hound wanted to go out, they simply stood in front of the door and emanated a silent extra-sensory message, that irrespective of where you were in the house, somehow trickled into your brain, and you found yourself obeying.

Returning to his tea ceremony his mind wandered back over the events of the previous night. He had never had such an experience. It was like being taken over in mind, body, and spirit. He had not impersonated O'Toole he had become O'Toole. To his astonishment he came to the realisation that he really was an inspiring and most excellent actor.

Pouring a second mug he began to dress. He only had a short window of time before the inevitable canine nagging began about it being 'walk time.' As he laced up his boots Moriarty entered and went through the bark and sign language routine that translated as, 'I want my walk now.' Scooping up the lead and poop bags the two companions embarked on the morning constitutional.

As Moriarty wandered from one pungent spot to another, digesting the smells left by other dogs and then adding his own unique signature to them, Nathan found his mind scampering back and forth trying to unpick and understand just what had happened to him last night. His success as O'Toole had stunned him. The applause and congratulations were overwhelming. He had felt so wired and excited by the whole thing that he had been overly wound up to stay overnight, and instead had simply driven straight back home to Southwold. Arriving back at two in the morning, he and Moriarty had crashed out on their respective beds.

He had never given a performance like it. For the first time in his life, he felt he had reached an almost transcendental level of acting. When occasion demanded he could become O'Toole. He pondered all this as various people stopped them and chattered in awe about Moriarty. He had replied to their questions and comments, but was frankly running on politeness autopilot. Arriving back at the apartment he sorted out Moriarty's breakfast and left him to it. His rumbling stomach prompted the manufacture of a bacon and tomato sandwich with more tea. Just as he finished the phone rang.

His agent's voice excitedly hailed him.

'You genius. You absolute genius. How did you do that last night? Watching it gave me goosebumps. It was like watching the real thing. You even looked like him. If I had closed my eyes, I would have sworn you actually were Peter O'Toole.'

Nathan found himself smiling.

'Well, you know I always had that in me. I just needed the right moment to bring it out. The real question is do you think I can get into the auditions now?'

Trelawney's booming laugh echoed down the line.

'Can you get in? Can you get in? My dear boy, their head of casting phoned me first thing this morning. He practically begged me to persuade you to attend the auditions. They want you at the Camberwick Grand Hotel Park Lane next month. You cracked it. Nine months ago, I thought you were crazy, not any more, old thing. You are now my number one client. I will send you the details as soon as I get them.'

The slight irritation at learning his agent had previously considered him crazy, was buried under the joy at getting into the auditions.

'I thought you always said I was your number one client?' Nathan queried.

'Don't be picky. You are my number one client.'

Nathan accepted a few more compliments and then rang off. Clutching an invisible partner, he waltzed like a latter-day Fred Astaire. With what he felt was exquisite grace he glided across the lounge. Reaching the door, he stopped. 'You shall go to the ball' he declared to himself. Buzzing and fizzing with excitement he jigged across the patio and onto the lawn and danced a perfectly timed hornpipe around Moriarty.

'Come on Puss we are going to London, and I won't become Mayor but I will become Peter,' he cried.

He couldn't quite understand why, but the look Moriarty gave him was the same as if he had just tried to borrow money from him. He didn't care. He was on his way to fulfil his dream.

24

THE RULING CLASS

The few weeks prior to travelling up to London for the auditions seemed to drag by at a pace that made continental drift appear a rushed and frantic affair. Nathan spent hours turning over in his mind how he should present himself at the audition. Should he go in dressed as one of O'Toole's film characters? Or perhaps an homage to an out of hours O'Toole, with a dark, classically cut sixties suit? Change his hair? Bleach it a little to emulate those blonde locks? In the end he decided to go as himself. In advance he carefully selected a pure white heavy cotton shirt, dark oatmeal-coloured trousers and a light tan jacket. He finished the ensemble off with matching tan leather moccasins. He felt it best to be himself and leave the O'Toole look, voice and performance until he was actually in the audition room.

Then there was the issue of whether he should attempt to sabotage any of his fellow thespians? Perhaps try to winnow out the field so to speak, eliminate some of his competitors, or should he simply trust in his own ability? "To be or not to be, that is the question?" Nathan's problem was his insecurity. Many actors struggle with this. Theirs was a life built around the instant feedback loop of applause from an audience. His desire to get this prize was so intense he was pressured to bend, if not shatter, the rules of correct behaviour. As a result, he was considering sabotage. His mind ran back over some of the somewhat morally dubious actions he had been involved in. The attempt to poison Lancelot, gaslighting Sammy, exacting revenge on Valentin. The twin spurs of ambition and insecurity drove him into this next heinous act. The sabotage of an audition full of innocent actors.

After much deliberation he prepared more of his patent laxative mixture. Some he placed in a few small envelopes, others, roughly half a dozen, were sealed in those paper tubes of sugar one gets in cafes. These he carefully opened, emptied their original contents and then re-filled them with the mixture and a little sugar. He then re-sealed them with the famous non-sticky sticky stuff. Secreting these in the pockets of his jacket he felt a little like Batman preparing his gadgets in his Bat-belt.

The next problem was Moriarty. He was determined they should continue this quest together. It stuck in his mind that each of the steps in his journey had all too often been successful because of Moriarty's input. Plus, in their time together they were never separated, ever. The problem was how to get him both onto public transport and into the audition. Nathan had booked a space at London's Crystal Palace Caravan and Motorhome Club Campsite for the week before the audition. Thereby giving them plenty of time to settle in. This camping site was the closest he could get the campervan to the Sheraton Hotel. It was however still some eight miles away, and the task of parking a campervan in central London seemed out of the question. He would either have to take a bus, train, or brave the Underground. The answer to this conundrum required some rummaging in the hall cupboard.

A few years back Moriarty had, as had often happened, been included in a television drama Nathan was working in. His role on that occasion was that of an assistance dog. For this the wardrobe department measured him up and produced a rather tasteful pale blue chest harness with the title 'Assistance Dog' emblazoned on each side in large friendly letters. A little research on the internet, courtesy of the local Library public computer, furnished Nathan with a couple of convenient legal loopholes.

First it seemed there was no actual register, digital or otherwise of dogs who were qualified Assistance Dogs. There was a requirement for them to be trained, after which they were issued with an ID, however it was illegal for anyone to challenge your dog's status, ask it to demonstrate its training, or even request to see the ID card. He resolved that if questioned he would answer carefully, although still truthfully, about Moriarty's status as his friend and supporter, his emotional rock as it were. Therefore, by selecting just how much information he would give, he could allow people to gain the impression that Moriarty was there to support him in staying calm, and not having a panic attack. The panic attack was actually beginning to look quite likely, especially considering the state of his nerves over the audition. Such flim-flam was not a difficult feat of verbal legerdemain for a professional actor of his experience. He even got grudging consent from his conscience. By comparison to some of his recent behaviour, his conscience felt this stretching of the law wasn't even worth mentioning.

Attiring Moriarty in his harness they did some test runs of the conversational deception using the local holiday makers as unsuspecting guinea pigs. If anything, the harness only served to enhance the level of attention Moriarty received, and left the hound slightly confused as to his sudden rise in popularity. He was quite used to being an object of fascination, even occasional adoration, but this new level of fawning admiration was on an entirely new level. He also couldn't work out why so many people kept telling Nathan he was very brave.

So, it was on a bright sunny morning the two companions set out on the next stage of their quest and headed for London. A latter-day Dick Whittington and Puss in boots. In this case, Nathan Stockwell and hound in harness. A Don Quixote and Pancho Sanza setting off to tackle their biggest windmill yet.

Arriving at the campsite after an endless series of twists and turns negotiating the camper van's bulk through the teeming streets of London, they arrived feeling a little careworn and stressed. Nathan enjoyed driving as a rule, but the sheer volume of vehicles reduced his transition of the streets of London to a joyless crawl. You know the traffic is slow when you get passed by the same jogger three times. If there was a circle of hell for overly ambitious actors he thought, this was it.

They spent the remainder of the day exploring their new home from home. It was a surprisingly large open green space, fairly close to the centre of London. Carefully managed greenery and footpaths gave them a restful haven from the bustling streets. Eschewing Moriarty's new harness they wandered around and unwound from the stress of travel.

They took the time to take the short walk up to the Sydenham Hill Rail Station. Nathan in his research had chosen that as the simplest way to get them to their destination. It would take them directly to Victoria station in just a quarter of an hour by overland train. Then it was only a short walk from there to the Camberwick Grand Hotel. He would of course need to allow additional time for this walk, as more people meant more stops for Moriarty to be admired. The one thing he was determined to avoid was the underground. The clue is in its title. The tube system by its very nature required descent into the ground and this meant escalators. Moriarty's one and only encounter with this particular infernal contraption had resulted in a sit-down strike, and a look that said 'you can't be serious.' Faced with an immovable wolfhound, Nathan had to finally pick him up bodily and hold him like a thirteen stone hairy drooling toddler, both for the descent and then again for their ascent at the other end. The resulting strain had meant he had walked funny for days afterwards.

The next few days were spent as a sort of impromptu holiday, and they bumbled about enjoying the sights of historic London. Clad in his fetching blue harness Moriarty seemed to have been granted his own personal 'get out of jail free' card. He was admitted without question onto the train and into every establishment they visited. Nathan never once had to deploy his carefully prepared back story. People just took it at face value.

On the day of the audition, they set off early. Nathan was determined to get there before anyone else. It wouldn't get him seen any quicker, each prospective candidate had been told to arrive by nine and then wait their turn, however he wanted to be able to assess the opposition at length. Therefore, he turned up at half eight.

Arriving at the Camberwick Grand Hotel in an unseasonal fog of sulky rain they were obsequiously ushered in by the top hatted, heavy wool coated commissionaire. He portentously touched the brim of his hat, and giving a quarter bow, held open the front door for them. They walked into the high arched lobby like twin lost souls, both gawping at the amazing luxury on overstated display. Like an homage to the lost opulence of the nineteen twenties, it was a riot of rich woods, gleaming stone, carpets your feet vanished into, and discreet strips of lighting, hidden, yet glowing. Having identified themselves at the reception they were directed to the lift and the aptly named Art Deco suite.

Coming out of the lift into a short corridor they approached the suite. Knocking timorously Nathan entered through the unlocked door. The suite's lounge had been adapted into a waiting room. Chairs were arranged across three walls, on the fourth was a table with insulated carafes of tea, coffee, loose sugar, a bowl of prepacked tubes of the same, and jugs of iced water. Nathan was relieved to find he was the first to arrive. He had even got there before the obligatory PA who would corral and shepherd the prospective actors in at the right time. He assumed the bedroom had been adjusted to serve as the actual audition space.

Wasting no time, he distributed his prepacked laxative sugar tubes on top of those already in the bowl. They had different colour printing and wording from the Sheraton branded ones, they were in fact emblazoned with the words 'Harbour Café,' but he relied on the natural human tendency to fail to spot trivial differences. The open sugar bowl was treated with a top layer of his unique powder blend.

He and Moriarty retired to the far side of the room and ensconced themselves in the corner. Moriarty after a short interval, realising nothing exciting was about to happen, and having already ascertained the woeful, and frankly inexcusable absence of any biscuits on the table, elected to lay down and catch up on his daily nap allowance. Twenty minutes later a harassed and stressed looking woman arrived. Her business suit and tightly clutched tablet marked her as the poor soul charged with organising the actors. She looked startled to find Nathan sitting patiently in the corner. She was even more surprised when Moriarty lumbered to his feet and padded over to make her acquaintance. Fortunately, she was a dog person and he got his required quota of admiration and fussing. Having established his position of prominence in the room, he returned to his spot in front of Nathan's feet, and resumed his nap.

Over the next few minutes various actors arrived. They each in turn would receive a greeting from Moriarty, take tea or coffee, then warily select a seat. All had decided to arrive a little before the designated audition start time. It seemed every one of them wanted to weigh up the opposition.

The film's producers had set the auditions to run from nine until one. Each prospective actor would have about ten to fifteen minutes before the next one would be wheeled in. Those selected to be shortlisted would be asked to come back for a longer session at a future date.

The room steadily became a disconcertingly weird conglomeration of men. Nathan looked around the room and experienced a slight sense of dislocation. It looked a surreal gathering. They were all of a type. His type. All were tall, over six foot. They were all lean. Not a spare tyre to be seen. Each sported O'Toole like cheekbones and blonde hair. Some had obviously elected to follow the hair tinting route that Nathan himself had briefly considered.

Then there was their wardrobe selection. Nathan was the only one who had dressed from his own personal wardrobe. Looking at the actors ranged around the room it was clear about three quarters of them had purchased a suit specially for the occasion. It was like entering a time warp. He was in a room filled with nearly identical men wearing nearly identical dark, well cut, stylish suits from the sixties. That time period he had always felt was the highpoint of perfect, smart tailoring for men. The elegant cut of the suits en masse highlighted the shabbiness of today's modern designs. Directly opposite Nathan sat Lancelot and Valentin. Both clad in identical suits they looked like clones. Lancelot gave Nathan a brief nod of recognition and a half smile. Valentin settled on a lip curling panto villain sneer.

The remaining quarter of the candidates had chosen to go the whole hog, and recreate a costume from one of O'Toole's movies. One had chosen the shabby dishevelled outfit from his "Pygmalion" as Professor Henry Higgins. Three had selected to come as Lord Chelmsford, in full Victorian military rig (complete with pith helmet) from "Zulu Dawn." On opposite sides of the room two king Henry the Seconds from the film "Becket" were glaring at each other with ill-concealed loathing. Another seated at right angles to them had chosen the older version of king Henry from the film "The Lion in Winter." He just looked embarrassed. A Don Quixote sat alone, uncomfortable and rigid in plate armour, evidently feeling "The Man of La Mancha" wasn't such a good choice after all. Finally, flanked by immaculate men in suits a lone "Lawrence of Arabia" stood out in flowing white robes.

Although Nathan felt dislocated by being among so many nearly identically dressed men, Moriarty wasn't confused at all. Dogs identify more by smell than sight. As humans we tend to change clothes constantly, at least from the canine point of view. We do however always smell the same. Moriarty greeted each new arrival in turn. Introductions complete, they would get a drink, then sit down as Moriarty catalogued them in his mind.

The room finally replete with O'Toole look-alikes, a long uncomfortable silence descended. Some of them obviously knew each other, but in the competitive atmosphere of the room the most they could raise was a nod, and a half smile would twitch across their features. More than half the candidates had added sugar to their drinks, either loose or from the little paper tubes. Nathan watched intently for the first signs of gastro-intestinal distress.

Just before nine the three movie executives arrived. Studiously ignoring everyone in the room they sailed past with an air of arrogant hauteur and on into the audition room. The PA consulted her tablet, running a well-manicured and painted nail down the list. Instantly the mood in the room tightened. Checking the time, she called the first name. An over excited besuited actor shot vertically out of his seat like a formally dressed jack in the box. Almost tripping over his own feet, he crossed to the door on unsteady legs and went into the audition room.

Over the next ninety minutes or so one actor after another went in to audition. Some were nervous, some had a confident swagger. However, in whatever condition they went in, they all had a similar dazed look when they came out. Nathan concluded that the three executives constituted what could be called a 'tough audience.' Some were in and out in just a few minutes, others lasted around fifteen minutes, but all looked haunted as they left the waiting room with silent despondent steps.

Just after half past ten the first effects of the laxative potion made an appearance. From various points of the room strange sounds began to be heard. A rumble here, a gurgle there, then the first victim to fully succumb became obvious. Don Quixote who had been squirming in his seat for some minutes was clearly in some distress. The metal breastplate he was wearing acted as a kind of impromptu, ad hoc echo chamber. The entire room were treated to the loud, hollow rumble and gurgle of his distressed stomach. He suddenly clutched his midriff in an attempt to both quiet it, and give himself some relief. As it turned out the breastplate prevented either of those things from happening. He wriggled a little more violently in his chair and swayed forward. Or at least as far forward as he could. Armour doesn't lend itself to bending over. With a final convulsive leap, he shot out of his seat and clattered to the door. Once again, the armour proved a less than helpful costume. Its inflexibility and weight meant he was less nimble and fleet of foot than he obviously wished to be. The sword in its sheath mingled dangerously with his hurrying legs. With a noise reminiscent of the tin cans tied behind the bridal car, he clanked rapidly away into the distance.

A moment later the latest actor to try his luck exited the audition room. Shoulders slumped he trudged wordlessly out of the waiting room. The PA called the next name. The younger of the two Henrys strode confidently across to the door, pausing only to cast a look of victory at his older self. Just as he reached for the door handle, he staggered, grabbed his stomach, and spinning round sprinted out of the waiting room. Judging by his speed Nathan felt he would probably overtake the clanking Don Quixote, who could still be heard staggering with tinny reverberations away into the distance.

Before the shocked PA could move to the next name on her list, three actors all surged to their feet one after another, and ran for the exit. First was Lancelot, impeccably attired in a black suit he headed for the door with an extended whimpering groan. A beat behind him was a second unknown, unnamed dark suited actor who also leapt into motion and attempted to pass him on the offside. Nathan was surprised by the late entrant to the lavatory two hundred metres. It was the Arabic robe clad Lawrence. He sprang upright and by sheer willpower and desperation elbowed his way between the other two. All three actors hit the doorway at the same moment in time. Lawrence of Arabia flanked by two dark suited O'Toole's. For a precarious moment they hung, suspended by each other's bulk in the doorframe. Legs pumping, elbows stabbing, torsos wriggling, they struggled to be free of each other. The white Lawrence sandwiched between the two black suits. They looked like an improbably large fabric Oreo. With an almost audible pop they exploded apart and legs staggering they careered across the corridor and attempted to regain some sense of balance. Lawrence lost his footing completely and disappeared down the nearby stairwell with a despairing wail, and a sequence of muffled thumps and thuds. The two others gave each other a look of frustrated loathing and then ran off in opposite directions. Each in search of the solace and sanctuary of the smallest room.

A stunned silence settled over the room. Eyes bulged in shock. Jaws dropped in disbelief. The PA took a slow deep breath. Today was not turning out the way she had expected. She consulted her list. Her lips moved in silent calculation as she endeavoured to work out who was supposed to be next to audition. To get an answer she needed to subtract the ones who had fled, then cross reference that with who was actually left. After a few seconds she reached a decision.

'Mr Stockwood, would you go through please,' she asked with all the fragile, porcelain dignity she could muster.

Nathan and Moriarty both stood up. They looked round at their rivals. A sea of tight faces and hungry eyes looked back. They stepped forward, pacing slowly across the plush carpet. Valentin glared at them in barely repressed anger. He was rocking back and forth. Bent half double and clutching his midriff. Nathan would have put money on him not being there when they came out.

With a light carefree smile on his lips, Nathan and Moriarty entered the arena.

The audition room was originally the bedroom of the Art Deco Suite. Today however it had been stripped of its usual furniture. In spartan style it now contained a long table behind which sat the director of the film, Davina Lean, the producer, Mungo Dexter, and an executive from the film studio, Serena Trunk. Facing the table and the inquisitors was one of those hideous hotel function room chairs. Its tubular grey metal legs framed a seat and back coated in a lurid purple and cobalt blue Dralon. It achieved the doubtful double combination of being totally bereft of any style or grace, as well as being utterly uncomfortable to sit in.

Nathan introduced himself and Moriarty, and sat in the rigid chair trying to look relaxed. After some initial surprise at the presence of Moriarty the three introduced themselves, and settled down to the business of assessing Nathan.

The producer opened a folder and began the process of reading out a resume of Nathan's acting career. Whoever they had doing the background checks was very thorough. It seemed they had dug up every performance he had ever given.

The producer started the inquisition.

'Looking at this I'm wondering why you were ever considered for gaining a shot in the audition process Mr Stockwood. Apart from the last year I would have said you were little more than a jobbing character actor. Competent enough in your own way I'm sure, but hardly capable of carrying such a big role in a major, major new movie.'

The director glared at the producer.

'You know perfectly well why he is here. It is because, I insisted he be here. I know he seems on paper to be an outside runner, but neither of you saw him on the Perkinson show. I did. It was nothing short of uncanny. I felt I was watching the real O'Toole. I have made the recording of that show available to both of you, but you clearly haven't taken the time to watch it.'

At this point the studio executive Serena Trunk weighed into the conversation with obvious anger.

'I've said this repeatedly, the studio is putting a lot of money into this film and if we don't get enough bums on seats, then we don't get enough bucks at the box office. I for one won't sign off on some unknown actor you seem to have taken a shine to, especially as it seems to be simply based on one appearance on just one chat show. It's too big a risk. Just wheel him out and get an actor in here with a name I recognise.'

Davina visibly bristled.

'Look, with this film we are trying to make something special. So, if you won't sign off on a competent actor who is probably perfect for the role, then I won't sign off on some talentless big shot actor, who has a name you know. Someone that you've hired just to boost your profit margin.'

From here the conversation went rapidly downhill. They first descended into a high-volume bitter wrangle over Nathan's suitability. Then the argument veered off into different territory. They spent some minutes on the personal capabilities and qualifications, or lack of them of each other. Nathan and Moriarty sat silent and stunned. The rift between the three seemed unresolvable. As the argument ebbed and flowed, it became more personal with each round. Nathan came to a decision.

He obviously had a staunch advocate in the director Davina Lean. Though at this point a good portion of her support for Nathan seemed to stem from her kicking back against having her judgement challenged. The producer and the executive were first and foremost money driven. No dough, no show. He needed to take control of the room and of the audition. In essence he had to act.

He closed his eyes and took one long deep breath. Then another. Looking inward he rifled through his store of O'Toole performances. Which one, which one? There. That one. It was from the film "The Ruling Class." The scene unspooled with the stuttering flicker of film clicking through the projector. It rolled into life in the private cinema of his mind. As it played, he felt the change coming over him again.

He shifted in his seat. He no longer perched, tight buttocked, uncomfortable and tense. His muscles relaxed and he now sprawled with confident ease. He watched the continuing spat for a long moment. A half smile twitched at the corners of his mouth. His eyes glittered with amusement. Moriarty suddenly looked up at him with startled eyes, he could feel the change, the shift in body energy.

With effortless fluid grace Nathan stood up. This unexpected action took a few moments to register with the trio of bitterly feuding movie makers. When it eventually sank in, their ranting slowly petered out, and they stared at Nathan in surprise. He waited until he had their full attention, he paused just one beat longer (for full dramatic effect), then he let them have both barrels. The crisp vowels of O'Toole's impeccable diction rattled toward them.

"My noble lords, the strong must manipulate the weak! That's the first law of the universe. The hard survive, the soft quickly turn to corruption. This is a call to greatness! Approach this day out to battle against your enemies. Let not your heart faint, fear not and do not tremble, neither be ye terrified because of them. For the Lord your God is he that goeth with you – to fight for you against your enemies, to save you. And mine eyes shall not spare, neither will I have pity. I will recompense them according to their ways, and their abominations that are in the midst of them. And they shall know that I am the lord that smiteth!"

The oration started strong and rose to a thunderous declaration that visibly rocked the audience of three in their seats. If you could take the performance power of O'Toole and bottle it, then Nathan had just drunk it. He didn't just speak the lines, he thundered them. He powered the dialogue across the room. His voice booming like an Old Testament prophet, newly descended from Mount Zion, bearing the unalterable word of Jehovah. Like sinners, they winced and cringed under the lash of his words.

The producer and the studio executive were open mouthed in shock. The director by contrast had a great grin plastered across her face.

'Well, you can skip watching the recording I gave you. That is what I was talking about. I think I have made my point, or rather Mr Stockwood has made it for me. Thank you for showing us what you can offer. If you are successful in reaching the audition shortlist, we will let your agent know.'

Without a word Nathan turned and strode confidently to the door, Moriarty padding alongside. As he turned the door handle, Nathan heard a faint unmistakeable voice whisper in his ear.

"Well done old sport, they won't forget that in a hurry."

Did he really hear it? Was it just in his mind? An effect of an overactive imagination? Just too much excitement? Honestly, he didn't really know, nor at that moment did he actually care

25

MY FAVOURITE YEAR

The following morning launched itself bright, clean and sunny on the Suffolk coast. A pre-sunrise shower had sluiced the promenade. Rinsed clear of holidaymakers it was left wet and glistening in the glittering early dawn light. Nathan stood sipping tea and staring out at the sun as it painted lurid, garish colours across the grey North Sea. It looked as though Jackson Pollock had vandalised a Lowry painting. He had been awake for over two hours now, just staring out, drinking tea and wondering what would happen next.

Of course, it all hinged on whether he got onto the short list. That now felt maddeningly beyond his control. His deployment of the laxative mixture at the audition had certainly disrupted several of his competitors. It had frankly reduced the auditions to something bordering on a farce, at least in the waiting room. In addition, it had hopefully inhibited several of his competitor's performances in this race for stardom.

Despite the bickering and rancour of the triumvirate of movie moguls, he felt he had put on an intense O'Toole performance. He couldn't better it. Now he just had to wait. Something he had always hated. The actor lives and breathes for instant gratification. They need immediate feedback. The Director yelling 'cut, it's a wrap.' The sense of a job well done. The praise of their peers. When on stage the feel of an audiences' mood bouncing back at you, and most of all, the applause.

His greatest consolation was that this time it seemed he was the driving force. His talent had been the deciding factor. Hopefully the decision would fall on the right side of the fence. This time it wasn't Moriarty who had impelled events and overridden his nefarious, Machiavellian plots. Like the cliched pavement artist with his masterpieces in chalk on concrete, Nathan could touch his forelock and say 'all my own work governor.'

It took another week for his agent to call him. By which time Nathan was more nervous than a long-tailed cat in a room full of rocking chairs. For days every time the phone crooked its electronic finger at him, he levitated upwards. Heart pounding, palms sweating, legs shaking he would gallop across the room to the phone like an inebriated, uncoordinated baby giraffe, only to sag in disappointment at yet another false alarm.

When he finally heard Trelawney's voice tinny and distant through the antique earpiece of his ancient Bakelite telephone, he felt as if his heart actually stopped beating. There was the inevitable awkward exchange of pleasantries and small talk, during which Nathan performed an impromptu jig from foot to foot. Finally, his agent got onto the only thing Nathan really wanted to know the answer to.

'Well, the movie people have finally got back to me.' He paused, waiting for Nathan to bite. You could almost taste his desire to get a response out of his expectant client.

Nathan said nothing, he knew any comment would only pander to his agent's sadistic streak. He would just draw the process out even further. This was especially true if what Nathan said betrayed even the faintest hint of interest. Best to affect a distinguished air of nonchalance. After an extended pause Nathan spoke. His voice heavy with bored disinterest.

"Really?'

He could feel the disappointment radiating out of the phone handset. Nathan one, agent nil.

'Yes, they had quite a lot to say.' A second pause, as once again Trelawney cast his bait before the hungry actor.

'Oh.' Nathan's tone shimmered with laconic boredom. Nathan two, agent nil.

'They had very definite views on your audition.' A deft thrust, the rapier of temptation shot forward.

'I'm sure they did.' Beat aside with an experienced parry, and Nathan held his stance. Nathan three, agent nil.

This tense ping pong game of bait and switch looked set to go on for some time. It was Trelawney's nerve that broke first.

'Look I will stop beating around the bush. The fact is …' He gave a final pause, unable to resist a last desperate attempt at tension.

Nathan had to bite the inside of his cheek to stop himself from rising to the bait.

The pause drew out. Finally breaking the silence and conceding the game of one upmanship his agent let loose a frantic hurried burst of speech.

'You are in. You have made the shortlist. There are only six of you on it. They want you back next month with the other shortlisted candidates for screen tests and a further in- depth interview. You will be required to be there for the whole day, and to be available at a moment's notice to be seen and assessed. On the plus side it's at the Camberwick again and this time you get the whole VIP package. All food and refreshments for the day, and the unlimited use of the spa facilities when you are not needed for screen tests and whatnot.'

Trelawney paused and took a deep breath before adding the inevitable negative point.

'On the downside, both Valentin and Lancelot are also on the shortlist.'

This was unwelcome news. Those two it seemed were destined to follow him through this process like an unwanted sweet wrapper stuck to his heel.

Nathan sighed. 'Well, I suppose that was only to be expected. Who are the other three candidates?'

'Well, they are all Hollywood names. They invited three higher profile actors to audition for the part. You and the other two from the London auditions will join them for the final round.'

'What!' Nathan exploded in horror. 'They can't be serious. It's a well-known fact that English actors can play Americans but not the other way round. Every time they attempt it, we get something risible. From Dick Van Dyke's dodgy cockney chimney sweep to Costner's excruciating Robin Hood with an accent that veered all over the dialect map of the UK. Often in the same sentence. It will be a disaster.'

'You are preaching to the choir, old boy. Apparently, they are part of the agreement the director, writer and producer had to strike with the movie studio. As it's an American studio that are putting up the bulk of the moolah, they made it a non-negotiable proviso that some bankable big-name stars were to be on the shortlist. Only two of them are American, the other is English.'

Nathan sighed. 'Oh well we will just have to go with it I suppose. I am sure none of them will be suitable. Who are they anyway?'

'Well, there is Mark Spencer.'

Nathan let out a hoot of derision. 'He's an action star, and he sounds irredeemably London East End. While I am sure it is a wonderful place, it has a lingua franca that does not lend itself to O'Toole's upper-class tones. On top of which he is bald.'

'Really Nathan for an actor you are at times terribly naive. There are such things as wigs and dialogue coaches you know. Next on the list is Spear Jackson.'

Nathan's voice went up several octaves. 'He's too short. Lovely chap I'm sure, but five foot seven can't play six foot two. Ludicrous.'

'Fair comment. Last one is Barrett Holland.'

Nathan reluctantly gave a grudging grunt. 'Actually, he's quite good. Right build and not too American sounding. Never seems to have done a bad film, and he's won an Oscar. Well, I will just have to work something out.'

Trelawney tried a drop of reason in an attempt to sway his client from anything rash.

'All you have to do is go in and do your best. I think you are perfect for the role.'

'Oh, I will do everything I can, but it never hurts to have an edge. An ace up the sleeve so to speak.'

'Please don't do anything stupid. I'm still not convinced there wasn't something fishy about that sudden outbreak of upset stomachs at the auditions. You didn't do something unpleasant did you?'

Nathan ignored the question. 'I will go down a couple of days before and get myself settled in and ready for the fray.'

The days leading up to the second round of auditions seemed to Moriarty to pass without incident. Nathan however, while calm on the outside, was internally feverishly creating and then discarding an unending series of plans. Moriarty and he followed their usual routine of pub, walks and loafing around. Despite the attempt at normality Nathan's stressed body odour gave the game away, and Moriarty deployed his usual tactics in an attempt to soothe Nathan's frayed nerves. This consisted of leaning his not insubstantial bulk against Nathan's leg. This invariably caused him to stagger. Moriarty would arrest the danger of Nathan falling over by standing on his foot at the same time, thereby accentuating the intensity of his support for him. This pose would be held until Nathan gave in and delivered a cuddle. This had the desired effect of calming his agitated friend. But even with this canine TLC Nathan still felt unsettled and edgy. The goal was in sight, but it could still slip away at the last moment.

He finally settled on falling back to his earlier method of psyching out the opposition. It had worked with Sammy in the panto, he just needed to find the right mental leverage to derail the opposition. Any excitable or high-handed behaviour would be frowned upon. Movies are a very expensive venture. No studio wants to work with a 'difficult' actor. They waste time, and time equals money. If he came over as competent and professional, while making the others seem like 'Prima Donnas,' he would present himself in a favourable light.

Nathan spent a week preparing his battle plan. To quantify it, and get it straight in his mind he decided he needed a 'Murder Board.' To be accurate it was really a 'Sabotage Board,' but the principle was the same. It would he felt, help him visualise each rival and pick out and isolate their weak spots. Unlike the psyching out of Sammy, this time round he had five different actors to undermine all at once. He could possibly set them one against the other. That way he could leave them to destroy each other. It would simplify the plan and minimise his own personal involvement. He could stand on the side-lines looking innocent, while the rest were throwing tantrums. To do this however he needed to know them and their weaknesses. Hence the 'Sabotage Board.' There was also the further problem of the short time frame. He only had the day of the audition to sow dissent and discord. This would require fine calculation and precise application to incite the actors to turn on each other.

Moriarty woke the next morning to find that during the night Nathan had cleared all the paintings from one wall of their apartment. Revealed in stark splendour was a blank expanse of ivory painted plaster. To this Nathan then began to fix five A4 photos of his rivals. These he arranged in a circle. Starting at the twelve-noon slot he had pinned Lancelot, then Valentin, Spear Jackson, Mark Spencer and Barret Holland. Underneath each photo he had attached a sheet of paper on which he intended to write his notes. He had already connected Lancelot and Valentin with a red cord. Mark and Spear were likewise linked. Two additional cords connected Lancelot to Spear, Mark and Barrett.

His reasoning was thus: Lancelot and Valentin detested each other, hence the red cord linking them. He also vaguely remembered hearing that Mark and Spear had never appeared in a film together. This led to some vague rumours they 'didn't get on' with each other. This in all honesty was most likely just so much celebrity gossip, manufactured by journalists to fill the insatiable desire of the public for tittle tattle.

Lancelot had an almost pathological dislike of all Americans and cockneys. Spear and Holland hailing from across the pond would automatically be on his hit list, as would Mark Spencer. He tended to be very open with his disdain of those he disliked. That should make it easy to drive a wedge between him and the others.

Moriarty sat, head cocked to one side, contemplating this dramatic new departure in Nathan's choice of décor. Up till now he had always been fairly conservative in his picture selection. This however was a radical new look. While Moriarty admired its boldness, it would not, he thought, catch on.

What Nathan needed to do now was more research into each actor and their foibles. Next stop the computer in the Southwold library. Equipping Moriarty with his blue Assistance Dog garb, the pair set out for the library.

Southwold library was an old red brick building. Constructed in nineteen hundred, it had over the years been used for a variety of functions. Initially the town Assembly Rooms, it was later a Roman Catholic chapel, a cabinet maker's shop, then in nineteen thirty-nine it became the Southwold library. Now in its semi-modernised interior, Nathan sat tapping away at the keyboard of the library PC with all the baffled unfamiliarity of a monkey poking a smartphone with a stick. Moriarty, with a masterly combination of friendliness, persistence and passive aggression, was engaged in gently bullying the hapless librarian into sharing his digestive biscuits.

Nathan skipped over researching Lancelot and Valentin. He felt he knew enough about those two already. It would take little work to have them tearing at each other's throats. Instead, he focussed his research on the three big stars.

First, Mark Spencer. Mid-fifties, average height but not too short to be ridiculous in the role. He seemed to perform almost exclusively in action films, often without a shirt. It seemed his lean physique was widely admired. He mainly seemed to appear in films that had more explosions than dialogue. His most successful movies had spawned a raft of sequels. The studio's reasoning seemed to be if the audience liked your first offering of cheese, more of the same would be swallowed, even it got consistently riper with each fresh serving.

Spencer had a well reported feud with Spear Jackson. Nathan could not find out why they were at loggerheads, or even if there was any truth in the rumour. He wasn't even sure if it was a real dislike or just something fabricated by the scandal sheets. Either way they both must be aware of the publicised rift, and should view each other with some uncertainty. It seemed most likely that they often did similar kinds of films, and they or the press thought that some kind of conflict was required. He decided to infer to each actor that the other had made some disparaging remark about the work of the other; that should pay dividends. Spencer looked as though he would not suffer fools gladly, and both of them had on occasion been abrasive with disrespectful journalists. That might play well. Certainly, it was worth a try.

Second, Spear Jackson. He was a hugely popular actor. That alone made him dangerous. He was a similar age to Spencer, but his height was a factor, he stood five seven. He should be far too vertically challenged to get the part, but you can never tell with movie studios. They had a tenuous grasp on reality at the best of times, and were quite happy to play fast and loose with historical accuracy. He was an exceptionally popular actor at the moment and his box office draw could sway the selection. There was also the danger of careful camera angles, and filming him while he was stood on a box to consider. His range of films was wider than that of Spencer. A number of quite well-respected movies, but he was most well-known for the 'Assignment Improbable' series. They were high octane action films famous for their outrageous stunts, all performed by Jackson himself. He was also famous for doing a lot of running in his films. Nathan watched a sequence of clips of the remarkable, galloping sprint he demonstrated in various movies. With a furrowed brow, he puzzled over why this was so remarkable. Everyone can run, more or less. He had even achieved it himself on occasions. When the situation called for it.

Planting fake comments in the ear of each, purportedly from the other could spark a conflict. Definitely on the merits of their respective bodies of work. All actors react badly to negative criticism on their performances. Whatever he did, he just needed to find some crack in both of their personalities into which he could insert the prybar of discord.

Third, Barrett Holland. He was tall, and a little older than the other two. He had a varied and impressive range of acting credits. His roles were what an Englishman might in their pompous way call more 'serious acting.' The films he had made were intelligent and successful. He had an Oscar win and multiple other nominations. He was clearly the main danger to Nathan securing the role. Frustratingly he seemed to be a genuinely pleasant chap. No scandal, no misbehaviour, on or off the set. He got on with everyone. He would be a tough nut to crack.

Nathan was interrupted by a distinct whiff of digestive biscuits as Moriarty came and peered over his shoulder at the screen. The Librarian had learnt the valuable life lesson that his new relationship with a wolfhound depended solely on his stash of consumables.

They returned to the apartment. Nathan carefully removed each sheet of paper from the wall. He made his notes, then refixed it under the intended victim's photo. He stood back and surveyed the pictures and their web of connections.

He now felt he had a plan of action to set them against each other:

Jackson and Spencer: by hinting about opprobrious comments about their films from each other.

Valentin and Lancelot: simply repeating some of the comments he had already heard them both make about each other's acting skills, or rather their lack of skills. That alone should light the blue touch paper.

Barrett Holland was the only one he could not find something to work with. Well perhaps something would occur on the day. In the meantime, he would continue to refine his scheme.

26

LORD JIM

As before, they travelled down early to London. Nathan had once again booked himself and Moriarty into the Crystal Palace Campsite a good two days before the audition. It was necessary for the preliminary stage of his scheme to get there well before the audition began. In addition to his plan to set the various actors at each other's throats, he had another scheme. A much more daring and dangerous plan. His obsession with securing the role of O'Toole meant he decided to leave nothing to chance. Therefore, before setting out, he had made a very precise and unusual selection of purchases, all of which were vital to this initial, high-risk stage of his plan. These items were now secreted away in another new purchase: a large black canvas military holdall.

They descended into the labyrinth of London. There the traffic performed its normal will sapping effect on Nathan. Vehicles ebbed and flowed with a glutinous snail like pace. He felt the time he spent waiting at junctions, waiting for lights, or just waiting for the traffic to even move, was actually far greater than his real traveling time. The denizens of London just accepted this state of affairs as normal. With the dead-eyed stare of a deceased cod, laid out cold and lifeless on a marble slab, they went about their half-lives. Nathan, coming from the hidden rural depths of deepest Suffolk found it soul destroying. Back home the biggest delay was the omnipresent tractor. These were invariably driven by farm workers who quite simply did not care how many cars were stuck behind them. Many of them were paid at close to minimum wage and so found comfort in the fact that although they were driving a tractor, they were still in front of you. But at least in Suffolk you all kept moving, albeit in a haze of slurry.

Once ensconced in their berth at the Crystal Palace Campsite, Nathan got Moriarty into his Blue harness. They then headed for The Camberwick Grand, in Mayfair. Phase one of his master plan required an onsite survey. To use suitably military parlance, he was there to reconnoitre. Despite his analysis of his rivals, and his planned method to pit them one against the other, he felt he needed just that little bit more. This character flaw repeatedly led him into deep water. What he had planned wasn't enough. There was one more high-risk strategy he could employ.

At every turn in this saga, he had struggled to rely solely on his talent, his abilities. His inbuilt insecurities had always led him to load the dice. He had to give himself an extra edge. Now as he stood on the verge of the final hurdle, he tried to give himself a double edge. He not only wanted to pit his rivals against each other, he wanted to know just what was in store during the auditions. If he knew just what the producers were looking for, he could tailor his audition to win their hearts and minds. To know that he needed to see the auditioners' notes. He envisioned the notes and information about the film would be in the film's executive penthouse suite. In the cinema of his mind it played out as an SAS style incognito incursion on the suite.

Standing on the opposite side of the road Nathan peered over the bustling traffic, and throngs of pedestrians, and scrutinised the hotel frontage with an intense, forensic stare. This part of his scheme was based on two overriding influencing thoughts. Both of these were based firmly in his past.

First. The childhood image of the Milk Tray man. In a famous series of commercials, he was seen dressed in a dramatic black ensemble. He scaled buildings to climb in a young lady's windows at night. Once gaining entry he did nothing salacious. He almost immediately snuck away again, simply leaving behind a box of Milk Tray chocolates, and a calling card embossed with his silhouette.

Second. Over the years of his career Nathan had appeared in far too many action films involving the special forces. Again, dressing in black was de rigueur. Plus, he got to play with the special equipment specifically chosen to enable the operative to fulfil his mission.

In short, he was imagining himself as a combination of James Bond and the cream of the SAS. His playing of a number of small non speaking parts as special forces soldiers far back in his theatrical past had fuelled his conviction that he could carry this off. Adding to this delusion was the knowledge that his mentor and idol, Peter O'Toole was, before fame struck him, a steeplejack. Throughout his life, when under the influence of one or two sherries too many, O'Toole would often scale the exterior of buildings. The man simply had no fear of heights.

There was a small whisper at the back of his mind. 'Are you sure you know what you are doing old sport?'

With the capable examples of yesteryear before him, Nathan's intention was to scale the outer wall of the hotel and effect entry into the penthouse suites at the top. He would then rifle the studio paperwork for the audition notes, and thus forewarned, and forearmed, he would be ready to acquit himself at the audition with full confidence. It never occurred to him that to simply walk in the front door, purloin a staff uniform and then enter without danger to life and limb was by far the safer option. Instead, he was fixated on the dramatic movie style entry. A modern re-enactment of the sixties heist film.

With this in mind he had procured the following:

1: Black canvas rope soled shoes.

2: Black cotton cargo trousers.

3: Black wool roll neck jersey.

4: Black wool beanie hat.

5: Black tactical leather military gloves.

6: Black nylon and cotton tactical vest with multiple pockets.

(You can probably spot the noir theme here).

7: Climbing hammer and crampons.

8: Climbing pickaxe.

9: Grappling hook and rope.

10: Military issue survival knife (just in case).

11: Military issue black coated torch.

As he studied the building, he put together a plan for the ascent. There was little or no purchase on the ground floor frontage. Smooth well jointed stonework gave him nothing to work with. However, there were a number of outside dining tables which had large umbrellas over them. These looked robust enough to take his weight. From the top of one of those he could reach the first-floor balcony. From there he would need to get to the third-floor balcony. However, to get to that floor he had a big problem. Like the first floor the third floor had a balcony. This time though there was a considerable overhang to negotiate. It was vital he reached the third floor. That floor, and the ones above, were where the suite levels were.

After some deliberation he decided it might be easier to cast the grappling rope from the first-floor balcony up to the third floor. If he could hook it over the balustrade, he could then climb the rope and attain the third-floor balcony. This would allow him access to the suites.

Moriarty sat bemused, wondering why they were stationary for so long. The building opposite was tasteful enough but didn't hold that much aesthetic appeal. He was at least entertained by a succession of passers-by who paused to both admire his magnificence and get a selfie with him.

After making copious notes and drawing a basic plan for his ascent of the façade, Nathan and Moriarty retired to the nearest inn for basic human comforts. Safely tucked in a corner table they ate and drank, while Nathan extended his notes into a step-by-step plan, complete with which items of equipment would be needed to complete each part of the ascent. His neuro diverse tendencies meant he could never resist drawing up a comprehensive plan.

Just after midnight Nathan, garbed in his new special forces outfit, crept from the van. In his hands he clutched a screwdriver and a roll of cling film. Once he was sure he was unobserved he swapped the number plates from his van with that of the elderly Volvo in the next pitch. His fear was the plethora of number plate recognition cameras that were dotted all over London. Swapping the plates should mask his true identity.

The cling film was a secondary level of protection. It may be an urban myth, but he had once read that cling film distorts the light and means the recognition cameras cannot accurately read the number plate. While he was sure he would be incognito, he wanted to make sure the innocent Volvo owner was, if possible, also free from retribution. Identity masking complete, he set off for the Camberwick Grand hotel. Moriarty jerked awake as the van set off. Night time drives were a rarity. Clambering to his feet he assumed his normal position and sat behind Nathan to observe their journey.

A discreet alley opposite the hotel, between a New Age novelty emporium and a RNLI Charity shop provided a safe place to reverse the van. With his usual scattergun mental processes Nathan filed their position in his mind as between the Devil and the deep blue sea.

Equipping himself with his various vests, gloves, and equipment had given him a sense of purpose and exuberant masculinity. He now slotted each item of specialised kit into one of the vest's multiple pockets. This raised his confidence several notches higher. By the time he slid his hands into the reinforced leather gloves and cinched their straps tight around his wrists he felt like a cross between Rambo and 007. Once he was set, he gave Moriarty a last hug. With the bright-eyed determined glint of a soldier going over the top he exited on his mission.

Moriarty watched in growing wonder as Nathan made his way across the road to the hotel. Nathan was fully in character now. He saw himself as the epitome of a super spy. As a result, he did not just walk across the road. Even men dressed all in military black would elicit little or no surprise. This was London. Instead, he was fully into the stealth character of an action hero. He flattened himself against the alley wall and peered round the corner. Watching the commissionaire amble back and forth, he waited for the moment the hotel guardian turned his back. Then he crossed the pavement in a sort of half crouched scuttling motion. Squatting behind a large four by four, he again waited till the commissionaire turned his back. Moriarty watched Nathan's bent knee pose scamper across the road with bemusement. Reaching the far side of the road he even executed a forward roll between two parked cars.

Nathan raised his head over the bonnet of the car just high enough to watch the uniformed gatekeeper surreptitiously lighting a clandestine cigarette. Timing his move to when the commissionaire looked away from him, he quickly crawled across the pavement on hands and knees and slid between the tables at the front of the hotel. There were three umbrellas each side of the main entrance. All were equipped with a large table with four to six chairs arranged around them. Nathan had chosen the middle umbrella, as he felt that would screen him best from the prying eyes of any late-night pedestrians.

It was here he encountered the first problem. Every time he tried to pull himself up onto the top of the umbrella it just tipped sideways towards him. It seemed even the weighty base was not enough to hold it steady enough to climb on to. Three attempts later he gave up on this approach. Carefully watching the commissionaire, he again waited till he turned his back. He then eased out a chair and scrambled up onto the seat and swiftly transferred his weight on to the back. This had to be done quickly as the chair was quite likely to topple over. Grabbing the edge of the umbrella fabric he transferred his weight, and with some puffing and limb thrashing finally got on top of it. The umbrella wobbled unsteadily, but stayed upright. Flattened on the canvas material he slid across until he was directly against the front of the building. The commissionaire wandered back and forth across the entrance in a bored nicotine clouded fug, blissfully ignorant of the night-time intruder.

As he turned and walked away, Nathan sprang into action. Standing on wobbling legs and with arms windmilling for balance, he reached for the balcony. As before, when he tried to pull himself up on the umbrellas, the natural instability of the structure came to the fore. The awning tipped alarmingly causing Nathan to flail his arms in ever more desperate circles to maintain his balance. Just when he thought all was lost, he slammed into the stone balustrade, bruising his ribs and winding himself. Clinging on frantically he clawed, sore and breathless, with frantic haste up and over the stonework. Rolling over the barrier he dropped onto the balcony floor with a muffled thud, and winded himself for a second time. The umbrella clattered loudly on its base as it righted itself. The doorman spun round at the unexpected noise and glowing cigarette in hand wandered down through the tables. He stood right under the pale and trembling Nathan who lay spreadeagled and panting on the balcony above. Frowning he looked round. Seeing nothing he shrugged and strolled back to the front door, taking a long meditative puff of his cigarette.

Nathan breathed a long sigh of relief. Moriarty had watched this clumsy farce in growing horror from the van, as Nathan continued with what the astonished hound could only surmise was some sort of nervous breakdown.

Once his breathing had restarted and the coloured dots floating in his vision cleared, Nathan stood up. With silent movements he deftly removed the grappling hook and rope from one of the many pockets of his vest. Coiling the thick cord loosely in his left hand he hefted the hook in his right. Leaning back out over the first-floor balustrade he gave the hook a couple of swings then tossed it in a perfectly aimed graceful arc upward, and missed the upper balustrade completely. The hook reaching its apogee tumbled back down and caught him right between the eyes. Blinded with pain he tottered for a moment and nearly went backwards over the edge. Rubbing the growing lump on his forehead, and cursing mightily under his breath, he pulled the hook back up on its rope, and prepared for a second attempt. This time his cast was successful. The curved metal prongs latched onto the third-floor balcony stonework. He gave the rope a couple of firm tugs to make sure it was secure. Then climbing onto the top of the balustrade he grasped the rope with both hands. Taking a deep calming breath, he began his ascent up the rope.

It quickly became apparent that he had forgotten just how difficult climbing a rope actually was. The fundamental principle of a hanging rope is that it is only attached at the top. As a result, as Nathan climbed it began to not only sway from side to side, but to twist. Nathan began to feel like a slowly revolving full-size action man pendulum. On the plus side the tactical gloves gave him good solid purchase, and his rope soled shoes allowed him to grip the cord with his feet. On the minus side was his life-long avoidance of any form of exercise whatsoever.

Searing pain set into his arms and shoulders at roughly one third of the way up. At the halfway point he quite simply ran out of strength. His burning muscles were just incapable of propelling him any further, either up, or back down.

Moriarty was perplexed by Nathan's stopping halfway up the rope. Up until this point he had to admit to being very impressed with his friend's hitherto unexpected athleticism on the rope. Nathan on the other hand was now struggling to even keep his grip.

The third-floor balcony was only just a few feet above him. Tantalisingly close, it swam in his sweaty, blurring vision. Muscles and joints protesting, he tried a few more upward heaves. Employing both his arms and legs in unison, he attempted with all his waning strength to get up the rope. It was useless, he was stuck (astute readers will remember that this is where they came in). He then suffered a horrifying flashback. Ten years old, gym class with the PE teacher, the sadistic one who really hated children. Off-white vest, baggy blue shorts, arms and legs like white pipe cleaners. The booming instruction, 'get up that rope you pathetic little weed.' He had only ever succeeded in getting halfway up. Now, hanging midway between his goal and possible death, he felt history repeating itself. Back in the gym of his youth, unable to go up or down he had clung there for what seemed an eternity while the teacher berated him and his lack of athleticism. Eventually he just fell off. Sadly, the same thing occurred now.

With a despairing wail he dropped, arms and legs splayed out he hurtled to the ground.

The commissionaire spun round and saw to his horror what appeared to be a guest caught in the act of suicide. Casting his dogend aside, clamping his top hat to his head, he vainly sprinted towards the falling figure. What could drive someone to take their own life by throwing themselves from the balcony? The errant thought that trotted across his mind was that they had probably just discovered how much they had spent on the minibar.

As fast as he ran, he knew he would never make it in time to catch the plummeting figure. Dropping through the night air, Nathan felt despair at such a stupid way to die. Moriarty hopped from foot-to-foot in frustrated anguish as his friend fell to certain death.

It was then Nathan hit the umbrella. Its wooden frame bowed and bent under the unexpected impact. The canvas stretched to near tearing point as Nathan's body slammed into it. It was at this juncture in the night's debacle that Newton's third law made another appearance in this narrative. To quote, *"for every action, there is an equal and opposite reaction."* Obeying the laws of the universe, the wood and canvas stretched down under Nathan's impact, then sprang back, the fabric snapped taut, and Nathan shot back up into the night air. Seeing the falling figure now ascending, the commissionaire ran even faster in an attempt to be the hero of the hour. Gravity began to reassert itself and Nathan's upward momentum slowed. For a heart-stopping breathless moment Nathan hung weightless at the peak of his trajectory. Arms upward the commissionaire reached out for the now once again descending Nathan. He missed. Nathan hit him squarely on the top of the head. They both cannoned back and down onto the floor, chairs and tables spun outward, clattering and splitting in all directions.

Nathan lay winded and dazed under a mortally wounded umbrella, the splintered remains of a chair giving his gluteus maximus an impromptu acupuncture treatment. The shock of the last few seconds meant he lay there stunned, winded and incapable of movement for some time. His dazed mind attempted to catch up with what had just happened. Finally gathering his scattered wits, he thrashed his way out from the clinging canvas and like a mariner clawing free from a shipwreck hauled himself upright. He limped away at his best speed across the road. Tumbling into the van he was greeted by the relieved and welcoming tongue of an excited Moriarty. Dropping into the driving seat he frantically started the van and shot off into the anonymous night.

The commissionaire, a sleeve half torn from his coat, a rip in one knee of his trousers, sat up with a groan. It took nearly five minutes to get his jammed and crumpled top hat off his head. Sight returned, he found himself alone. Pulling his abused body upright he stood, a solitary figure among the shattered debris of the furniture. He looked in vain for the suicidal guest. It slowly dawned on him the great difficulty he was going to have explaining all this to the manager. His boss was a famously unforgiving personality. Taking a deep philosophical breath, he tottered back to the front door to resume some semblance of his normal routine.

That settles it, he thought, the next jumper is on his own.

27
BECKET

It was a bruised and crestfallen Nathan who rolled wearily and stiffly from his bed the next morning. Scattered across the floor were the various accoutrements of his night time raid on the hotel. He looked at them with a feeling of faint disgust. They were painful reminders of an ill-advised venture. The whole thing had been an absolute disaster. What had he been thinking? Acting the part of an SAS hero in some TV drama does not give you the required skill set to do it in real life. It only means you can look as though you know what you are doing. In the end it's all make believe. Like many before him, he had swallowed the dream he had created on screen and made it real in his mind. It's not real, it's just going to the dressing up box and playacting.

Still, on the bright side apart from some minor bruises and a severely dented ego he was otherwise intact. Not everyone falling from what was almost the third floor of a building could make that boast. He limped towards the kettle and started the early morning ritual of making the very necessary tea.

Moriarty watched him through half lidded eyes. To his relief his friend seemed to have returned to his normal self. Last night had been disconcerting to say the least. At first, he had wondered if this was part of some film, but the absence of the lights, cameras and the other associated technological paraphernalia had soon dispelled that notion. Now he was simply happy that things seemed to be back to normal again. He still resolved to watch Nathan very closely, and make sure he headed off any future aberrant behaviour.

Hot mug cradled in cold fingers Nathan opened the door and stepped out into the crisp early morning sunshine. Moriarty a step or two behind. A surreptitious glance assured him the number plates on the adjacent Volvo were correctly re-affixed. It had been his last job before he had wearily clambered into the van and collapsed on to his bed. He had been so shocked and tired when he got back that he had momentarily worried that they might not be the right way up. Moriarty leant his comforting weight against Nathan's hip. The shared touch gave positive reassurance.

An hour later, both replenished with bacon and tomato sandwiches (in Moriarty's case bacon and bacon sandwich) the pair set off for the audition. Nathan dressed smartly but casually, Moriarty in pastel blue Assistance Dog vest. The auditions were to be held over a whole day. He would be interviewed, screen tested and asked to perform a short piece before the three auditioners. The movie company had booked out the entire Spa section of the hotel for their exclusive use.

They arrived at the same time as Lancelot. Meeting right outside the front door Nathan was forced to go through the pantomime of seeming to be pleased to see his rival. It was unthinkable for any Englishman of his generation and class to ever appear ill-mannered. Walking in together they spotted Valentin registering at the front desk. Taking his ID lanyard, he turned and glared at the two approaching actors, and large shaggy hound. Apart from his frosty stare he made no sign of welcome or recognition. Shoulders hunched in tense hostility he stomped off towards the Spa.

The two actors gave each other a frowning, conspiratorial look.

'Looks like we are off his Christmas card list this year,' whispered Lancelot.

'I didn't even know he had a Christmas card list' replied Nathan with a confidential grin. 'After all he would actually need to have some friends to have a list.'

Getting their ID's, which included one for Moriarty (who accepted his lanyard with a suitably grave expression, one more in keeping with being given the Victoria cross), they set off towards the looming audition. A short anonymous corridor led them to the rear of the hotel. The Spa door, opened into the large machine filled space of the Gym. Through a curved glass wall, the heated lozenge of the outdoor pool sparkled and glittered with sunlit reflections. At the far end of the pool an alfresco bar area had been equipped with tables and chairs loaded with a selection of refreshments. A smartly dressed young lady approached, resplendent in high heels and a very tight pencil skirt, and equipped with the obligatory tablet. She welcomed them with a professional smile and ticked them off her onscreen list.

'Food and drinks are at the far end, near the bar,' she declared, 'you will be required to be available all day today. We have set up two of the exercise studios for your interviews and screen tests.' She handed them each a slim folder.

'In here are the lines for the scene they want you to deliver. So, you will need to learn these please. You will be called individually when you are needed. If you wish to use any of the Spa facilities please do so, just let us know so we can call you when we need you. I hope you have a lovely time with us.'

She finished with a brittle smile overflowing with all the tremulous insincerity of a woman expecting at least one of these actors to be difficult. Nathan reflected that if he had his way, five of them would be very difficult.

Casting a quick eye over the scene typed out in the folder, Nathan felt his confidence rise. It was taken from a film that was very familiar to him. He knew this part inside out. His performance should present no problems. He just needed to throw a spanner in everyone else's efforts.

Doing the most natural thing for actors they both took immediate advantage of the free food and drink. Valentin clutching a coffee kept himself as far as possible away from them. Just a few minutes later the director Davina Lean and the producer Mungo Dexter came out of the nearest exercise room, crossed the gym and joined them outside. Taking their time they circulated among the three actors, shaking hands and slapping shoulders in a decent attempt at bonhomie. Their goal, Nathan supposed, was to put the actors at ease and help them slide comfortably into the audition process. The studio executive was notable by her absence. As the corporate face of the film, she obviously felt no need to make friends. In silent recognition of their mutual rivalry, the actors had all drifted a little away from each other. This allowed them an area of private space to talk with each of the two auditioners.

Davina was the first to chat with Nathan.

'I'm so glad you are here. You have probably already worked out that you are my first choice for this role. But, before you get too excited, remember you have to convince the other two as well.' She looked at him with an open infectious grin. Nathan beamed in response. He gave his most confident yet still ever so slightly humble smile.

'Yes, I know. I'm just grateful for the chance to be considered,' he replied.

A few more comments, and a little mutual praise was exchanged, then Davina headed off to chat with Valentin.

Mungo Dexter was next. He gripped Nathan's hand in a bone crushing handshake. Pumping it vigorously up and down he used his free hand to give Nathan a solid buffet on the shoulder.

'Well done,' he boomed. 'You probably have already guessed Davina is struck with the idea of you for the part. Frankly, I wasn't so sure. Don't get me wrong, you gave a great performance in the room, but what swung it for me was your Assistance Dog. Anyone who is willing to expose themselves like that is someone exceptional. I have been in therapy myself for years, and I know how difficult it can be to be upfront about your anxieties. You weren't just upfront, you absolutely owned it. Making no secret of your dependence on this wonderful dog is incredibly brave.'

Here he paused and gave Moriarty a vigorous rub on top of the head. The rest of what he said flew past Nathan without really being taken in. He was blown away by this revelation.

Internally Nathan was reeling. Just a few days ago he had been congratulating himself on getting onto the shortlist on his own merit. Now he knew it was Moriarty that once again had tipped the scales of fate. He had got in on a two to one vote because he had an Assistance Dog. He looked down at the instrument of his destiny, Moriarty gazed back with the innocent brown eyes of a blameless, albeit hairy, cherub. Despite the disappointment of being upstaged again, he still felt mightily comforted by having this faithful companion with him.

There was still no sign of their three high-profile competitors, so Nathan decided to begin sowing his seeds of discontent among the two actors already there. Dropping into a chair next to Lancelot he leaned over and whispered, 'well I didn't expect that.'

LSD shot him a worried look. 'Didn't expect what?'

Nathan gave an exaggerated glance left, then right. 'It seems our favourite villain, Valentin has been trying to influence the auditioners against us. It looks like I'm pretty well tarnished in their eyes already. As for you, the producer is still undecided, and could go either way in his view of you. Valentin has told them you are very unreliable as an actor. Apparently, he's put it about that you are something of a Diva. Always late for shoots and constantly making demands.'

'What' exploded Lancelot, 'me, unreliable? I'm a professional through and through. Devious little ingrate. I'm not standing for that. Well! He will be sorry he slandered me, just you wait and see. This means war.'

Nathan gave him a reassuring pat on the arm. Standing up he sauntered off towards the food table where Valentin was loading a plate with sausage rolls. Lurking just out of kicking range a drooling Moriarty watched with covetous eyes. Picking up a sausage roll, Nathan deftly flicked it towards the hound. Moriarty went up on his hind legs and expertly snapped it from the air with all the grace of an outside leg fielder snatching the ball.

Valentin peered at him with a look that, for the first time ever in his life Nathan could only describe as being inspected with a gimlet eye. His eyebrows rose steadily in surprise as Nathan nonchalantly dropped into the chair alongside him. The eyebrows went back down as he returned Nathan's cheery smile with his customary glower.

'Whatever you want to say, I don't want to hear it, you can clear off to your little luvvie chum over there,' he growled.

Nathan painted a look of mystified surprise over his features. 'Oh, sorry, it's just I thought you might want to know what Lancelot has been saying to the auditioners about you. I know there isn't any love lost between you and I, but I don't like to see anyone stabbed in the back. Even you. It's just not my idea of what gentlemanly conduct should be.'

Nathan put both hands on his knees, and began to rise with a weary, injured dignity. Valentin's arm shot out and grabbed Nathan's bicep, yanking him back down into the chair.

'Hold on. What has that toadying little twerp been saying about me,' he hissed.

Once again Nathan did his exaggerated mime of looking over first one shoulder then the other. Leaning forward he began to whisper.

'Well, and this really must stay between the two of us, you know, just between you me and the gatepost as they say. It turns out he has been dropping comments about your alleged limited acting range.'

Valentin sat bolt upright as though a broom handle had just been deftly shoved up the back of his shirt. His face went a deep beetroot red, and he puffed up like an incensed gorilla who has just seen his rival eat the last banana.

'Limited acting range.' The voice escaping through his rage constricted throat was reduced to a hoarse falsetto. 'Limited acting range,' he repeated, an octave higher, as though saying it twice would make the whole preposterous idea vanish.

'Yes,' confirmed Nathan. 'He has told them you are a one trick pony. You can only do the Victorian melodrama cad. You know, moustache twirling caricatures of villains, and he says that even those are one dimensional and unconvincing.'

If asked Nathan would have said it was impossible for Valentin to sit any straighter or get even more red faced; he was wrong on both counts. The broom handle had now sprouted a second section at right angles to the upright pole; the shoulders squared and stiffened. The face already considerably larger than normal now swelled further, and took on the appearance of a puffer fish about to do itself a mischief.

Swallowing several times, he finally regained a modicum of composure.

'Do you think they believed him?' The question contained a vulnerable note of insecurity.

Not only insecurity. More than that. To Nathan it revealed the chink in Valentin's armour. The reality was that he actually was a one trick pony, and deep in his heart he knew it. Whatever acting skills he may have started with, had long been buried under years of playing the successful persona of a charismatic thug. A part he had portrayed over, and over again. The subtlety of his acting craft had disappeared under years of exaggerated panto villain performances.

'No.' Nathan said with palpable insincerity. 'I'm sure they have seen the full range of parts you have played.'

This dig got right under Valentin's skin. You could almost see the thought processes running across his synapses, as the hideous truth dawned that his career had been pretty much a one note song. For one moment the fragile, vulnerable ego that lurks under the skin of every actor stood naked and revealed in the spotlight. Then, the dominant part of Valentin's naturally pugnacious personality rose once again to the surface. Like an angry shark his temper reasserted itself.

'Well, he's picked the wrong person to challenge. I won't stand still for lies like that. This means war.'

Nathan heaved himself to his feet. Then through the glass wall he saw the first of the American contingent arriving.

Barrett Holland was greeted by the trim young PA. She handed him the folder and rattled off her prepared welcome speech and list of instructions. Folder in hand he wandered over and through the glass door. He introduced himself to the three actors with genuine cordiality, and shook hands with the two auditioners. As he circulated and chatted Nathan found himself internally grinding his teeth. The man was just simply too pleasant. He seemed to have no ego for Nathan to exploit in this convoluted mind game.

An audible rattle and crash heralded the arrival of Spear Jackson. The slight, smartly dressed actor seemed to literally bound through the door. His every movement radiated an annoying level of enthusiasm. Greeted by the PA, he gave her an overly long and intrusive hug, then trotted towards the pool and the gaggle of actors, clutching his folder. Ready to mingle with his rivals, all of whom he was determined to make into his new best friends.

His sheer exuberance was already starting to grate on Nathan's English sensibilities. As Jackson bounded from one to the next, pumping hands, slapping shoulders and grinning like the Cheshire Cat, Nathan experienced a feeling akin to nails being slowly dragged down a blackboard. He held his fire for now, and checked his tongue. He needed Spear Jackson's alleged arch nemesis, Mr Mark Spencer, to be here before he launched into the next stage of this plan. Fortunately, he didn't have long to wait.

This time the door inched open slowly and the face of Mark Spencer peered suspiciously into the Gym. Slowly, he pushed through the door. Approaching the PA with a deadpan expression he listened impatiently to her rehearsed welcome speech, then snatched the folder from her hand. He then continued to ignore her till she wandered away, blushing with awkward embarrassment. Spencer stood for a moment, taking in his surroundings, then sulkily read through the sheet in the folder. Finishing, he folded it several times, and stuffed it into the back pocket of his jeans. He then behaved as if he was the only person in the audition, and studiously took no notice of everyone.

The two auditioners withdrew and the actors briefly carried out a short mingling dance of forced camaraderie. Eventually the enthusiasm for this wound down, and they slowly gravitated to separate parts of the room and settled into an off-centre orbital arrangement.

This final motif was delineated by their perceived relationship to each other. This, in turn was then informed by the minutiae of their relative connections (or lack of them) and their individual personality traits, and ultimately decided where they eventually chose to sit and wait for the call.

Valentin sat the furthest apart, alone, scowling and hunched.

Mark Spencer came next in the distancing stakes.

Nathan and Lancelot sat together but with a solitary chair between them. United, but apart.

Barrett Holland also sat alone although apparently unconcerned by this fact, and with a Zen like absence of any stress.

Spear Jackson was incapable of sitting still for long at all. He periodically shot out of his chair and settled next to one or the other of the collected actors, and launched into an animated discussion. Whether he was welcomed or ignored seemed to make no difference whatsoever to his enthusiasm level. As much as he seemed to like everyone in the room (Mark excepted) he particularly loved Moriarty. As an exceptional hound Moriarty took adulation in his stride, however this level of animated adoration amazed him. After giving Spear a few eye-rolling stares, he settled down and just accepted it for what it was. Worship.

Some twenty minutes later the PA teetered into view, Tablet in hand she despatched Valentin into the first interview and Holland off to the first screen test. The others sat scrutinising the audition part they would have to perform, while surreptitiously eyeballing each other over the top of their folders. The exception was Nathan. To make it look like he was trying to memorise the part he pretended to read it intently. In reality it was a scene he knew by heart.

Nathan thought that the selection was most likely that of the film's director, Davina. She had already shown herself a fellow fan of O'Toole's work. The piece chosen was the opening scene from O'Toole's 1964 epic "Becket." The film is something of a forgotten masterpiece. In its day it had won an Oscar and had been nominated in eleven other categories. In addition, it had won three BAFTA's and been nominated for four others. On top of which it had both won and been nominated for a slew of other awards. Today though, this magnificent film has faded into semi-obscurity.

The film started with an opening scene that was actually the end of the story, the narrative then jumped back to tell the rest of the tale from the beginning. It was this difficult, edgy opening soliloquy the auditioners had chosen for the actors to recreate.

About half an hour passed in relative silence; then a door banged open. It swung outward so violently it bounced back and almost hit Valentin on the rebound as he stormed out of the interview. He stamped back into the pool area then spun round and with dramatic gesture pointed at the stunned auditioners who had followed him out of the room. They stood huddled in a shocked cluster in the Gym.

He held this theatrical pose for a beat, then bellowed,

'You talentless hacks wouldn't recognise a truly gifted actor if he bit you in the leg. How dare you judge me. I wouldn't appear in your cheap tawdry home movie if it was the last acting job in the world.'

With a defiant gesture he kicked the pool door open in a final demonstration of rage, and strode away. There was a stunned silence that went on far too long for anyone to be really comfortable with. The assembled actors stood open mouthed at this highly dramatic scene. Their minds whirled as they tried to work out what had happened in the audition room to spark this burst of anger. Nathan just inwardly smiled at this first successful ousting of a rival. Moriarty just stared at Valentin's abandoned plate of sausage rolls. He had just been contemplating that if Valentin was busy in the other room, then was there a possibility that they were, for the sake of argument, going to be available to any passing hungry wolfhounds. Now that Valentin had stormed off, the prospects for that looked very favourable.

At this point an oblivious Barrett came out of the screen test room dressed in full Lawrence of Arabia white robes and shouted.

'You guys are going to love the screen test. Look at this. I adore this outfit,' he cried.

The silence that greeted him tipped him off to the fact something was wrong.

'What? Did I miss something?'

Mark was next for the interview and Lancelot for the screen test. Spear sat with Nathan and absent-mindedly stroked Moriarty.

'What was all that about?' he asked.

Nathan shrugged. 'Your guess is as good as mine. You know what it's like. Some actors are just very highly strung. They get an idea in their head and nothing can shake it out of them. It's like you and Mark. I understand from the press you two don't get on.'

Spear nodded in unhappy agreement. 'I don't know where that story came from, but it seems to be everywhere. In reality we've barely ever spoken to each other, but these constant rumours seem to have made us both a bit suspicious of each other.'

Nathan again performed the twin shoulder look around routine. 'Well, I heard it's that he thinks your films are just crass, shallow, unbelievable action trash, full of impossible stunts and more explosions than dialogue. Whereas his films are realistic, gritty action dramas that reflect the violent fractured modern society of today.'

For a moment Spear looked stunned. His mouth literally hung open. Then with a visible shaking he pulled himself together. His eyes for the first time blazed with something other than excessive camaraderie.

'Unbelievable. Do you know I perform every stunt myself? No stunt doubles, no CGI cop-out. Pure realistic film making. Old school movie magic. His films on the other hand are just paint by numbers action flicks. The plots don't even make any sense. Characters do stuff with no reason or logic. All so they can finish it off in some overblown final showdown scene. Arrogant, strutting idiot.'

Nathan nodded in sympathetic agreement. 'I've found some people just can't deal with anything they perceive as a threat to their own particular body of work. Between you and me I am surprised he is here at all. You are right, his CV is rather over full of high-octane action epics. Not really the sort of film that would lead him naturally to the biopic of a classical actor. Doesn't really make sense to me I'm afraid.'

Spear nodded vigorously. 'I get what you mean. Apparently, he wants to break the mould. Did you know we both have the same agent? He gave me the inside track on what Mark is thinking. It seems he is determined to prove he can do the deeper roles. Plus, he is no spring chicken. He can't keep doing these full on, crash bang movies much longer. Frankly, I'm the same. I keep myself in good shape, but honestly, it gets harder every year. I, unlike him, have done a much broader range of films. I can crossover into the quieter more thoughtful roles. Truth be told I probably am not the right choice for this particular part, but I want to give it a go. It's a challenge.'

Nathan found himself warming to the man. On some levels he could still be annoyingly upbeat, and exhaustingly jolly, but at his core he was sincere. It was hard not to like him, even with that big cheesy grin of his.

Lancelot edged sheepishly through the door from the screen test and shuffling across the gym, he joined the two of them. Nathan grinned at him.

'How was it? Did you love the costume as much as Barrett?' queried Nathan.

All three of them glanced at the lone actor who now sprawled in a nearby chair, legs stretched out, gently snoring.

Lancelot gave a sheepish slightly embarrassed look.

'Frankly it was a bit off putting for me I'm afraid. The chap running the screen tests is a bit old school. He insists on complete and utter realism. As a result, I had to strip right off before putting the outfit on. I moaned a bit but he told me there were no underpants under the garb of an Arab chief. I mean it's not as though anyone could even see my pants under those robes.'

Nathan threw his head back and roared with laughter. He had forgotten Lancelot had such a strong puritan prudish streak. It had been the butt of many a ribbing while they were on tour in the smaller theatres with communal dressing rooms. All the women in one and the men in another. Lancelot had been so shy about undressing he had gone through acrobatic convulsions trying to get into his costume without revealing too much sordid flesh. Nathan had constantly referred to it as his 'dance of the seven veils.'

The door to the interview room opened, and Mark stepped through with a heavy tread. His face and demeanour gave nothing away. He exited looking as grave and irritable as when he had entered. Ignoring everyone else he poured himself a drink and retreated to a chair on the far side of the pool, the one furthest away.

Next Lancelot was summoned to the interview room and a moment later the PA called Nathan to the screen test studio. He stood up, and with Moriarty in tow entered his first arena. Moriarty, a veteran of filming, found a quiet corner and settled down to watch.

The director in charge of the screen tests was a small twitchy man who bubbled with suppressed energy. He bustled back and forth brandishing a tape measure. He swiftly determined, and noted Nathan's dimensions. Then, tape cast round his neck like a 1940's Savile Row tailor, he fussed and tutted along a rack of white Arabic robes. Muttering inaudibly, he flicked along the rail till he found the closest match. Unhooking it he spun it back and forth to look at every angle.

'Yes, yes, this one. Not perfect, but close enough. Right strip off. Everything! I'm not going through another argument about underpants,' he commanded.

Nathan just looked at him steadily and with a suitably serious face took the costume from him.

'Of course. Authenticity is vital.'

Lacking Lancelot's shyness, he simply retired to a corner and stripped. Carefully folding his clothes and stacking them on a chair. Then without a trace of coyness, despite the fussy leader of the troupe, two cameramen and one lighting woman, he slid the long white robe over his head. As it settled over his long frame, he could feel the essence of O'Toole sliding into his marrow with a sensation both warm and cold at the same time.

Next, he strapped on the broad belt, complete with curved knife with its gold-topped white ivory handle. On top of that he slid his arms into the cream sleeveless top robe. A long white scarf was next, he carefully wrapped and arranged it around his head. Finally, the gold roped headdress that held it all in place.

The screen test crew were watching in an awed silence.

'What?' Asked Nathan. 'Have I missed something?'

'No, no. It's just it looked like you had done that a thousand times before. It's perfect. We took ages getting the other two into the outfit correctly,' replied the puzzled director.

'Really? It just seemed right to me. I didn't really have to think about it.'

Nathan stepped forward into the bright curved arc of the spotlight. The two camera men poised themselves behind their instruments. One was running a movie camera, the other snapped away with an HD still shot device.

Nathan stood for a moment as the two men moved in opposing arcs around him. Cameras digesting and storing every detail. Then he remembered a story about O'Toole when he was first filmed in this identical outfit. The director David Lean had asked him to improvise, it seemed there was nothing in the script, other than "Lawrence admires himself in his costume." A solo scene, just Lawrence, for the first time alone in this stunning regalia. Understanding he was playing a young man wearing these flamboyant robes for the first time, O'Toole had played up to that. Nathan did the same. With the film scene running like a movie in the bioscope of his mind he spun, first one way, then the other. The robes swirled and shimmered around him. The fabric twisted around him in dazzling white swathes. His body matched and linked with the movements of O'Toole playing in the picture house of his memory. Finally, he stopped, standing tall and confident he whipped out the knife from its sheath and admired his reflection in the mirror bright steel.

Moriarty, watching crouched and silent in his corner had risen to his feet. He gazed in awe at his transformed friend. Once again, as had happened more than once in recent months, this metamorphosis had manifested itself. Nathan stood an alpha male, a true pack leader.

The Director and his crew had their mouths hanging open. Just for a second, for the merest whisper of time, they could have sworn the echoing space of the exercise studio had vanished. For a moment, just a bright, fragile moment frozen in temporal limbo they had been in the hot baking desert as this tall, elegant man spun and twirled in his magnificent robes. The sun burning, huge and golden. The sky a searing bright, white blue. The sand smooth and yellow spread around them.

Nathan stopped and looked at them.

'How will that do?'

When Nathan and Moriarty went back into the poolside bar, they found the atmosphere was less than relaxed.

Lancelot was sitting looking traumatised after his interview. It presumably had not gone well. Nathan knew from past experience with him, that when he felt threatened or challenged, Lancelot could become rather strident. He attempted to dominate any group he was with, even if (as in this case) they were meant to be vetting him. Planting the thought that he was being labelled as difficult meant that once in the audition room, he would be, well, difficult.

Mark and Spear sat at opposite ends of the bar area. They glowered at each other with resentment and animosity lurking at the back of their eyes. Nathan felt his comments to Spear had borne fruit. Before he had been attempting to befriend everyone. Now with the thoughts of Mark's antipathy towards him running through his mind, he stared with as much truculence as his rival. It seemed just raising the actually non-existent spectre of their supposed feud had made it real.

Barrett alone seemed relaxed and calm, as he tucked into a large salad.

As it was now midday Nathan loaded two plates with consumables. One for each of them. Moriarty padded alongside him looking pleased with Nathan's selection of high protein treats for him.

The three auditioners now made an en masse appearance and helped themselves to the selection of food. It was not the most relaxed meal. They sat spread out, not engaging too much with each other. Once all had finished, the three made the rounds of the waiting actors. A word here, a handshake there.

Spear brightened up and regained his cheerful demeanour.

Mark looked stern and shook hands with sober, serious dignity.

Lancelot mumbled replies and looked embarrassed.

Nathan and Moriarty worked together as an impeccable double act to schmooze the auditioners.

Barrett alone seemed naturally relaxed. So far, he had seemed to gently waft through the process of the audition without any visible stress.

Now it was Mark to go for the screen test, while Nathan, took a deep breath and entered the audition.

As before the three executives sat behind a long table, while a solitary chair was placed facing them. The furniture was slightly different from the earlier first audition interview, though still of the same bland type. An uninspired, anonymous design favoured by hotels around the world.

He scanned the assembled faces trying to read their mood. Davina leant forward, looking keen and ready to start the process. The producer Mungo Dexter gave him a tight half smile. Serena as the studio money representative just scowled.

Davina Lean started the ball rolling.

'Well, the purpose of this interview is for us to get to know you as a performer and a person. Mungo and I will be working very closely with you if you land the role. Serena, as the studio representative here, is to look after their substantial investment. She holds the purse strings so to speak.'

Nathan nodded. He decided to only say what was necessary, that way there was less chance of foot in mouth disease.

Mungo chipped in next.

'Exactly, it's not just finding out if you are right for the part, but we need to know if we can work with you. These days movies are a very expensive undertaking. We need to know not only if you can fulfil the role, but how well you can work with us and the crew. This interview will help us see how quickly we can get the project 'in the can' so to speak.'

Serena leant forward, putting both elbows firmly on the table.

'Unlike my associates I don't go in for tact, so I'm just going to say this out loud. I need to know two things. One, can you carry a big part like this in a major production. Given your B list career so far, I have some serious doubts. Two, will having you in the role affect the box office. Again, your B list career counts against you. The studio head honchos have told me they are very keen on a bankable 'name' in the title role. No offence, but you have got to really sell yourself to me if I am going to bring you on board.'

Again, Nathan nodded. It was his experience that whenever someone said 'no offence' the next sentence was inevitably offensive. This was certainly true here. He could have bristled and blustered, but that was not the right play here. So, he decided least said soonest mended. His plan was to answer only specific questions. If he stuck to what they wanted to know with zero extraneous information, he felt he had a better chance of swinging the decision in his favour.

Davina glanced acidly at Serena. She cleared her throat.

'Let's start with the basics. We saw you give an outstanding O'Toole impression the other day, but why should we select you for the role?'

Like a game of tennis Nathan watched this first question come floating over the net. He too cleared his throat, and gently lobbed back the answer.

'None of you really know me. Serena is right, my career has been pretty much B list for most of my life. But it wasn't always like that. You see I initially became an actor because of Peter O'Toole. I not only wanted to be like him, I wanted to be him. For me he ignited the screen in everything I saw him do. Watching him was the closest thing to a spiritual experience I have ever had. I dedicated my life to knowing his every role inside out. Like him I trained at RADA, just so I could walk in his steps.'

'However, along the way I somehow lost that zeal. I became successful enough to be comfortable. Admittedly B list comfortable, but comfortable nonetheless. I rose to a certain height in my profession, and stopped. I was content there, happy even. Then you came along and changed my life.'

All three of the auditioners frowned in bewildered unison.

Serena tipped her head to one side.

'We changed your life? How? I hadn't even heard of you till Davina started banging on about how you were our O'Toole,' she queried.

Nathan chuckled. 'It's like that cliché about a butterfly beating its wings and starting a hurricane. You simply decided to greenlight this film and post an advertisement in The Stage announcing the auditions. That was my "Road to Damascus" moment. Your advertisement literally changed my life. In an instant all my old ambitions were reborn. The old forgotten fire in my gut burst into new life. It was like a phoenix rising from the ashes.

Thanks to you, I am a new man, or rather I am the old man returned to life from the dead. You see, I know in every cell of my body that I was born to do this. None of the other actors waiting out there can do this the way I will. My whole life has just been an apprenticeship leading to this room, this one moment in time. Therefore, I have decided that I will help you in your decision. Every question you ask me from now on, will not be answered by me. Instead, Peter O'Toole will answer. You see I don't just know his performances, I know him, all of him. From this point on you are not interviewing me, you are interviewing Peter O'Toole.'

'You need to understand that along the way to here, to right now, I have changed. I've done things I never thought myself capable of. The last twelve months have been a rollercoaster journey. I'm not even sure the man before you today, is the same one who read your advertisement all those months ago. What I do know is that this is my role. It does not belong to anyone else. No one can do this the way I will. I just have to convince you.'

Saying this he sat back in his chair and closed his eyes. Looking inward he opened his mind to the persona of Peter O'Toole. Moriarty stirred beside him. His fur bristled as he sensed the change. It wasn't some kind of supernatural possession. It was as if Nathan slid into an element of his persona that had always been there; a facet that was as much part of him as his own skin. Now however, he let it rise to the surface, while the rest of his own personality sank from sight. It slid out of every pore and altered him.

Nathan opened his eyes and took a long slow breath. He lost the stiff tension of an aspiring auditionee, and sprawled back in the chair, relaxed and commanding. He crossed his long legs with an elegant grace. He folded his arms over his lap, wrists crossed over each other. The fingers of his right hand held an invisible cigarette. Head bowed he looked at the three through half-lidded eyes. To their confusion he raised the non-existent cigarette and took a long inhalation. Blowing out illusory smoke he sat back, and waited.

The silence drew out. The three exchanged looks of puzzlement. Then Mungo broke the moment with the first question.

'Why do you think you are the right person to play this role?'

He tapped ash from the imaginary cigarette. Raising his face, the intense cobalt eyes fully opened and pinned them to their seats. The long slow drawl of O'Toole flowed over them. The voice of a totally relaxed, in control man. Tones of warm chocolate covered with a crisp layer of upper-class diction.

"It's my job, it's what I do, it's what I'm on earth for and it's who I am."

Next Davina spoke. 'What will you bring to the part, how will you play him?'

There was a brief pause; Nathan/Peter considered.

"I will not be a common man because it is my right to be an uncommon man. I will stir the smooth sands of monotony."

This threw them for a moment. Three quizzical faces peered back at him. Then Davina and Mungo nodded as understanding dawned. Serena frowned for a few seconds then slowly replaced it with a half-smiling, half puzzled expression, and a hesitant nod.

Serena recovering from this enigmatic answer fired a question of her own.

'Do you feel you can rise to the occasion of a major role like this?'

Nathan threw back his head and released a staccato bark of laughter.

"Acting is largely a matter of farting about in disguise."

Serena let out a growl of annoyance at this answer, while the others both struggled to hold in their amusement. Nettled by this charade she threw a second question.

'Why do you think a second-rate, B list character actor like you can play Peter O'Toole?'

Nathan/Peter smiled with all the confident condescension of the true artist. He threw his arms wide and said,

"The reason angels fly is that they take themselves lightly."

Davina let out an uncontained burst of mirth. 'OK, OK. I think we have been far enough down this rabbit hole for now. When you came into the hotel you were given a scene form one of O'Toole's films. Can you perform that for us?'

Nathan/Peter unfolded his arms and legs and stood before them. He slipped off his shoes and socks. Next his jacket slid off and was draped over the chair. Then the shirt, button by button was undone and removed. Bare foot and bare chested he walked with the slow sensuous steps of a ballet dancer to the front of their table. He folded down onto his knees and clasped his hands together.

Serena whispered with urgent haste from the corner of her mouth.

'What the heck is he doing?'

Davina threw a quick irritated glare back at her and whispered with curt irritation,

'Why don't you watch any of the films O'Toole made. He's recreating the opening scene. The film starts at the end of the story, then jumps back to the start. He is being King Henry kneeling before Becket's tomb.'

Here as your narrator, I must interject. I cannot in mere words on a page even hint at the power of the original performance, nor even that of Nathan's repeated version. You need to see and hear it for yourself. Suffice to say it ran the gamut of emotions. Angry, sad, melancholic, resentful, petulant, despairing, nostalgic, determined, wistful.

"Well, Thomas Beckett. Are you satisfied? Here I am, stripped, kneeling at your tomb, while those treacherous Saxon monks of yours are getting ready to thrash me. Me – with my delicate skin. I bet you'd never have done the same for me. But – I suppose I have to do this penance and make my peace with you. Hmm. What a strange end to our story. How cold it was when we last met – on the shores of France. Funny, it's nearly always been cold – except at the beginning, when we were friends. We did have a few – fine summer evenings with the girls. Did you love Gwendolen, Archbishop? Did you hate me the night I took her from you, shouting "I am the King?" Perhaps that's what you could never forgive me for. Look at them lurking there, gloating. Oh, Thomas, I'm ashamed of this whole silly masquerade. All right, so I've come here to make my peace with their Saxon hero because I need them now, those Saxon peasants of yours. Now I will call them my sons, as you wanted me to. You taught me that, too. You taught me everything. Those were happy times. You remember, at the peep of dawn, when as usual we'd been drinking and wenching in the town. You were even better at that than I was."

The three auditioners each experienced this performance in a different way,

For Serena, the hardnosed executive, it was just a half-naked actor kneeling in front of the table, and doing a competent job of being Peter O'Toole.

For Mungo, Nathan's performance was spellbinding. The dialogue rattled and hissed across his consciousness like jolts of static. When it finished, he came back to reality, to the here and now with a physical jolt and jerk. He had been swept away by the sincerity of the acting.

Davina had what can best be described as an out of body experience. For her the brightly lit exercise studio faded away. She found herself actually in the crypt, sitting next to Becket's tomb. Nathan himself morphed into O'Toole. The very air in the room changed into the cold damp of a subterranean, stone clad space. At the back of the room, she could even glimpse the shadowy forms of the waiting monks. They lurked with petty glee, waiting to chastise a king. Even the faux wood of the table altered. She could quite literally see the carved form of Thomas Becket laid out across its surface in ghostly shadows.

Nathan stood back up, turned and dressed himself. The shimmering body language of O'Toole slipped away and Nathan resumed control of himself. Properly clothed he turned back to face them.

'Any other questions?'

The three all shook their heads.

'No,' said Davina quietly. 'I think that will be all for now.'

Moriarty rose. Together the pair headed for the door.

'Wait,' called Serena, 'do you truly believe you are the actor to play this part?'

Nathan paused. His hand was frozen halfway to the door handle. When he turned back to face them, he wasn't Nathan, he was once again Peter.

"I'm not an actor, I'm a movie star."

He turned back to the door and flung it open and stepped out into a scene from bedlam

Nathan and Moriarty never found out just what or indeed who started the fight, but when they left the audition room it was definitely in full swing. All the participants were in enthusiastic action. Mark and Spear held each other in a squirming, wriggling dance of hold and counter-hold; living proof that real brawls are nothing like movie fights. There is no choreography, just a sort of clumsy wrestling. They staggered and shuffled around the edge of the pool. Barrett Holland circled the struggling grunting actors like a referee, shouting for calm. In the opposite direction Lancelot also went round, waving his arms ineffectually and making small bleats of horrified panic.

It was a small miracle, and perhaps testament to Nathan's charisma, that the fracas had gone unnoticed until the point he opened the door.

He and Moriarty trotted forward to help break up the squabbling actors. Nathan tried to prise Spear's arms from Mark, who was trapped in a headlock and slowly going purple. Moriarty fussed around the edge of the fight looking for a space to intrude his bulk into the fun. The PA squeaked and cried out in shrill tones for the fight to stop.

A combination of things now brought the affair to its inevitable farce-like climax. Nathan, with one mighty heave succeeded in yanking Spear's arm away from the wheezing Mark. The unfortunate PA was hit mid-chest by his arm. The fact that she was dressed in the height of current fashion meant she was wearing a tight, figure-hugging pencil skirt that only allowed her to move her legs from the knee down. To add to the inevitable outcome at this precise moment Moriarty was right behind her, as was the vast open expanse of the pool.

The out-flung arm collided with her chest. She squawked in shock and tried to step back to regain her balance. Because of the ridiculously tight skirt and high heels, and her attempt to avoid the large Irish wolfhound, she took a dramatic pitch backward and somersaulted into the pool. The scream and splash had the desired effect of finally terminating the struggle. Barrett helped haul the soaked, complaining young lady from the water. Her tablet gave a few flickers, and sinking to the bottom, went to the final eternal home of all abused technology.

The three auditioners slowly walked in. They looked in horror at the disaster zone.

A soaked and dishevelled PA was telling everyone exactly what she thought of them, and that she would sue the lot of them.

Barrett was quietly trying to calm her down.

Mark and Spear were trying to rearrange their clothing and regain some decorum, while still glaring at each other.

Lancelot had collapsed into a chair and was having a fit of the vapours, and weakly calling for brandy.

Nathan had been knocked off his feet and sat stunned on the floor.

Moriarty, seeing the fun was over for the moment, was doing his best to tidy things up by eating all the food that had been knocked onto the floor.

28

MASADA

It took just over two weeks for Nathan to find out if he had been successful in achieving his goal of securing the coveted role. Seventeen days of nervous twitching, and toe tapping impatience. Moriarty later looked back on it as a low point in their life. He could see Nathan just wasn't himself. Distracted he went through the motions of their usual routine, but his heart wasn't in it. He was present in body but not in spirit.

For a fortnight he jumped and rushed to the phone for every call. When Trelawney his agent finally rang with the news, he was so dispirited and worn out that he just stared at the phone for several rings before listlessly picking it up.

'Nathan Stockwood here,' he said with a voice redolent with despondency.

A tinny voice rattled and squeaked out of the earpiece.

'I thought you would be permanently sat by the phone waiting for the result. You took so long to answer I nearly gave up,' his agent said with audible petulance.

'Sorry. After this much time with no news whatsoever, I just sort of got a bit fed up of rushing to answer every telephone call. I'm guessing you must have the result, unless this is just a social call,' sighed Nathan.

'Oh, I have the result alright. Are you ready?' he teased.

'Go on, get it over with.'

'The runners and riders from last to first are...' Here he gave a long pause for dramatic effect.

'In last place, Valentin. His tantrum ruled him out of the process straight away. They were glad to see the back of him.'

'Next: Lancelot. Apparently, he had some sort of hysterical meltdown during the interview and harangued them about how he wasn't a Prima Donna, and he would sort out any one of them who accused him of that sort of behaviour. All three were completely confused by this rant. They just couldn't understand it, they had not at any time in the process accused him of such behaviour. Again, the verdict was that they felt he was going to be more trouble than he was worth.'

'Neck and neck were Spear Jackson and Mark Spencer. Their box office draw meant that the studio liked the idea of using one of them, but didn't think it worth the risk. That bout of fisticuffs they had made them pretty much untouchable. Even the studio's representative wouldn't countenance them in the role.'

'Which left you in second place.'

Nathan let out a sigh of resignation.

'I guessed Barrett Holland would get it. I shouldn't really be surprised. The allure of a box office name was bound to be irresistible.'

A delighted chuckle rippled down the line.

'Hold your horses, don't count your chickens, it isn't over till the fat lady sings, and a stitch in time etcetera. Wait for it. Drum roll for dramatic tension.' Again, the overlong pause.

'He turned it down!' shouted an ecstatic Trelawney.

His yell was so loud Nathan snatched the phone away from his ringing ear. Then the shock of what he had just heard kicked in and took the strength from his knees. Stumbling he dropped into a chair. He sat there panting, eyes bulging, limbs trembling.

'Say that again,' he whispered.

A second deeper chuckle followed.

'He. Turned. It. Down.'

For a moment he couldn't breathe. His fingers trembled so much he almost dropped the receiver.

'It's me? Me? I've got the part? Why? What happened? Why did he turn it down?' The excited words tumbled out. His tongue tripping over itself in excited haste.

'Well, it seems he just feels he isn't right for the part. He gave no other excuse or reason. He just thanked them for allowing him the chance to audition and then simply dropped out of the process. So, unless they are willing to start the whole audition process again, you have it.'

Nathan just hung up. Some miles away in his Norwich office Trelawney looked at the phone handset in surprise and accusation, he shouted Nathan's name several times down the phone mouth piece before hanging up with a muttered, 'actors, they are all crazy.'

Nathan sat without moving or talking for nearly an hour. Moriarty was concerned and wandered over and butted him with his head a few times to no avail. Eventually deciding Nathan needed a full on no holds barred comforting session, Moriarty turned round, backed up, and sat on his knee. Apart from a stifled grunt of pain, Nathan gave no sign he was there. After some time, the wolfhound owner's reflex kicked in, and he began to absent-mindedly stroke Moriarty's great furry back. Moriarty, with the zen like calm of the wisest sensei sat and received his stroking, secure in the knowledge that this time-honoured therapy would work. Eventually.

Some hours later, with the new and startling information that he had, against all the odds achieved his goal slowly percolating down into Nathan's cortex, the two friends gently strolled along the promenade. Late in the day the sea whooshed and hissed in lazy ponderous surges over the flints of the Suffolk shore. Seagulls bickered and strutted. A few errant scraps of litter tumbled in the late afternoon breeze. The last of the summer visitors took a final look at the heaving grey North Sea and headed for their accommodation.

Both hound and thespian were surfing through their own ponderings.

Moriarty was running back over the last year. It was without a doubt the most eventful time of their lives. They had been involved in some quite exceptional dramas. They had made new friends, and seen and done some very surprising things. He felt Nathan had changed quite dramatically. The alpha dog side of his personality had surfaced several times, something Moriarty had seldom seen. On another level Moriarty felt he had been involved in some great saga, the full meaning and outcome of which lay just beyond his grasp. He knew he had somehow been instrumental in influencing great events, but he wasn't quite sure how he had done it. He gave a mental shrug. In the end it didn't really matter. They were both together and were still happy. Whatever had happened and whatever was about to happen that simple fact would still be true. Their relationship with its myriad layers of complexity and nuance would continue. Despite all of it he still completely understood the importance of being Moriarty.

Nathan was also in the process of roaming his own personal mental landscape. What a year this had been. He had come so far. He had done so much. He had committed such crimes.

He had poisoned multiple actors. He had gaslit several others. He had even tried his hand at breaking and entering. Before he had seen that audition notice in The Stage, he would never have contemplated such heinous deeds. None of this was, for want of a better phrase, 'in character.'

The thing that was now getting under his skin, and itching like a rose thorn, was that now he had achieved his goal did he really want it? He had done things he wasn't proud of. He had hurt and manipulated innocent people, some of whom he really quite liked. Was it actually worth the price?

He had pursued it because he was obsessed with the importance of being Peter. Considering everything, he now wasn't sure he was really like Peter at all. Not as a person. O'Toole had always been centred in himself. His supreme self-confidence carried him over and through every obstacle. He was a man with a towering ambition. Nathan had only become that way himself in pursuit of this goal. He had in fact put himself to one side in the pursuit of being someone else. He had submerged his own personality.

He looked down at the great shaggy bulk of Moriarty padding alongside him. Perhaps he should be more like Moriarty. Wolfhounds stalked through life with all the awful majesty of an Emperor. Their utter self-confidence and complete certainty of being, made them impervious to all of life's trials and challenges. Yet they did so with a calm dignity that just allowed them to float through life stress free.

The further thought that getting this coveted role was ultimately down to his hound was also staggering. Throughout this odyssey the tipping point always seemed to have been Moriarty. Every time. Even in just small ways with minor actions he had always somehow managed to derail the hurtling steam train of fate.

Moriarty had pushed Deidre onto the stage and thereby set off the human dominoes that ultimately pitched Lancelot into the orchestra pit and out of the show.

In the panto, after all Nathan's work and planning, it had been Moriarty who had morphed into Black Shuck and petrified Sammy into a hysterical breakdown and put Nathan into the key role.

Valentin, with his allergy to dogs, meant Moriarty was the instrument that effected the role change that got him that breakthrough television role.

Even after his magical rendition of Sonnet eighteen in the interview, it was Moriarty, who with stately grace strode onto the set, and with scene stealing skill placed a great clawed paw with tender care on Esme's knee, and the crowd rose to their feet and went wild.

When it came to the audition shortlist, he had only got in by a two to one vote because the producer had, like so many in our modern world, been in therapy himself. With that background he had softened to Moriarty as Nathan's 'Assistance Dog' and had voted him into the final six.

It occurred to him that the ruse of putting Moriarty in the blue harness had in actual fact been anything but a ruse. It was subconsciously acting out a very real and self-evident truth. Moriarty wasn't just his dog. He really was Nathan's assistance dog, his therapy dog. He was his brother. He was family, more so than the human ones whom he rarely saw.